Train the Trainer

The Art of Training Delivery

Second Edition

By
Skills Converged

Copyright © Skills Converged Ltd. 2016

All rights reserved. No part of this publication may be reproduced, stored in a retrieval system or transmitted by any form or by any means, electronic, mechanical, photocopying or otherwise, without the prior permission of the Author (publisher)(copyright owner).

No responsibility for loss caused to any individual or organisation acting or refraining from action as a result of the material in this publication can be accepted by the Author.

The right of Skills Converged Ltd. to be identified as the author of this work has been asserted by them in accordance with the Copyright, Designs and Patents Act 1988.

Skills Converged® is a registered trade mark of Skills Converged Ltd.

Skills Converged Ltd. is based in London, United Kingdom

A CIP catalogue record for this book is available from the British Library.

Library of Congress Control Number: 2016911366

Published by CreateSpace Independent Publishing Platform, North Charleston, South Carolina

ISBN-13: 978-1534611085

ISBN-10: 1534611088

Cover Design: E. Honary

Book's Website: www.SkillsConverged.com

Available as paperback and on Kindle.

2.9

Contents

FOREWORD -- **9**

1 WHAT CAN YOU LEARN FROM AWFUL TRAINING COURSES? ----------------------- **11**
    1.1   WHAT IS THIS BOOK ABOUT? -- 13
    1.2   WHAT YOU SHOULD PROMISE TO DO -------------------------------------- 13
    1.3   TERMINOLOGY: WHO ARE DELEGATES? ----------------------------------- 14
    1.4   TERMINOLOGY: WHAT KIND OF TRAINING? --------------------------------- 14
    1.5   HOW TO AVOID POOR TRAINING DELIVERY -------------------------------- 15

2 WHAT DOES IT TAKE TO BECOME A GREAT TRAINER? -------------------------------- **19**
    2.1   WHY A TRAINER'S EXPERTISE CAN BE A TURN OFF -------------------- 20
    2.2   WHAT SHOULD TRAINING BE CENTRED ON? ------------------------------ 20
    2.3   KEY PRINCIPLES IN ADULT LEARNING --------------------------------------- 22

3 WHAT IS ACCELERATED LEARNING? --- **27**
    3.1   THE HISTORY --- 28
    3.2   THE SETUP OF THE ENVIRONMENT --- 30
    3.3   THE GUIDING PRINCIPLES -- 31
    3.4   ACCELERATED LEARNING TECHNIQUES ----------------------------------- 33

4 HOW TO PLAN YOUR TRAINING -- **39**
    4.1   WHO ARE YOUR DELEGATES? --- 39
    4.2   WHAT DO THE DELEGATES NEED TO LEARN? ------------------------- 39
    4.3   WHAT DO THE DELEGATES ALREADY KNOW? -------------------------- 40
    4.4   HOW MANY PEOPLE ARE YOU TRAINING? ------------------------------ 40
    4.5   WHERE IS THE VENUE? -- 41
    4.6   WHAT ARE YOU TRYING TO ACHIEVE? ------------------------------------- 41
    4.7   WHAT RESOURCES DO YOU NEED FOR THE TRAINING COURSE? -------- 42
    4.8   HOW WOULD YOU EVALUATE THE TRAINING SESSION? --------------- 42
    4.9   WHAT ARE THE HOMEWORK OR POST-COURSE ACTIVITIES? -------- 43
    4.10   HOW TO EVALUATE YOUR OWN PERFORMANCE --------------------- 43

5 WHAT IS TRAINING NEEDS ANALYSIS? --- **49**
    5.1   HOW DOES TRAINING NEEDS ANALYSIS WORK? ------------------------ 50

	5.2	Training Needs Analysis Data Collection Tools	51
	5.3	What Are the Stages of a Training Needs Analysis?	52
	5.4	Training Plan	53
	5.5	Aim to Learn from Feedback to Enhance Your Training	55
6	**What Are the Critical Principles of an Effective Training?**	**59**
	6.1	Didactic Principles	60
	6.2	How to Avoid Barriers to Learning	62
7	**What Is the Ideal Training Environment?**	**67**
	7.1	What Are the Standard Equipment in a Training Room?	67
	7.2	What Not to Do	70
	7.3	How Lights Can Make All the Difference	71
	7.4	Keep the Training Room Ventilated to Avoid Sleepiness	72
8	**How to Select an Ideal Training Room Configuration**	**77**
	8.1	Classroom	78
	8.2	Boardroom	78
	8.3	U Formation	79
	8.4	Two Perpendicular Lines	79
	8.5	Backward Perpendicular Lines	80
	8.6	Circular Formation	80
	8.7	Circular Table	81
	8.8	Half Circle	81
	8.9	Group Exercises	82
	8.10	Interview Position	82
	8.11	Informal Chat	83
9	**How to Start a Course**	**87**
	9.1	Handling the Silence Treatment	87
	9.2	Make People Feel Comfortable at the Start of the Course	88
	9.3	Use Team Building Techniques as a Warm Up	90
	9.4	Start a Course Like a Movie	90
	9.5	Do Not Apologise for Being Boring	92
10	**How to Increase the Impact of Training Exercises**	**95**
	10.1	Your Proficiency When Running an Exercise	95
	10.2	Managing Delegates During Exercises	96
	10.3	Managing Exercise Difficulty	97
	10.4	Handling Groups When Running Exercises	99

Skills Converged

11 HOW TO MANAGE ENERGY AND PACE — 103
- 11.1 An Uninterested Trainer Is Utterly Boring — 103
- 11.2 Positive Attitudes Are Contagious — 104
- 11.3 How to Spot Unmotivated Delegates — 104
- 11.4 How to Motivate an Audience and Avoid Boring Them — 107
- 11.5 What Is an Ideal Pace? — 108

12 HOW TO MANAGE EXPECTATIONS — 111
- 12.1 How to Empower Learners — 112
- 12.2 How to Exceed Expectations While Learning — 114
- 12.3 The Gap of Disappointment — 119

13 HOW TO MANAGE ATTENTION — 125
- 13.1 Attention Span — 125
- 13.2 Manage Energy, Not Time — 127
- 13.3 Chunking — 129
- 13.4 How to Raise Interest and Gain Attention — 130
- 13.5 What to Do During the Breaks? — 131
- 13.6 Types of Attention — 132

14 HOW TO MANAGE LEARNING — 137
- 14.1 The Great Brain Transformation — 137
- 14.2 Allow Delegates to Make Mistakes — 140
- 14.3 Don't Use External Rewards for Motivation — 141
- 14.4 Cognitive Disfluency — 143

15 HOW TO BE A MASTER PRESENTER — 149
- 15.1 Express Yourself Concisely — 150
- 15.2 Use the Summary Sandwich Technique — 152
- 15.3 How to Avoid Making Poor Expressions — 152
- 15.4 Body Language Plays a Critical Role in Your Training Performance — 154

16 WHAT IS THE SECRET IN KEEPING DELEGATES CONSTANTLY MOTIVATED? - 157
- 16.1 The Anatomy of a Course — 157
- 16.2 How Can You Add Structure to a Hands-on Course? — 159
- 16.3 What to Start with: Lecture or Hands-on — 160
- 16.4 How to Optimise Your Training Approach — 161

17 HOW TO INCREASE THE IMPACT OF TRAINING USING STORYTELLING — 165
- 17.1 Do Stories Matter? — 165
- 17.2 What Can Storytelling Do for Teaching? — 166

17.3	The Fox, the Cat and the Wolf Have Taught Us So Much	167
17.4	How to Tell a Good Story	168
17.5	Engaging Introductions	171

18 WHY ASKING QUESTIONS CAN SIGNIFICANTLY IMPROVE YOUR TRAINING COURSES — 175

18.1	Case Studies	176
18.2	What Is Happening in all of these Training Courses?	177
18.3	What Is the One Thing You Need to Consider?	178
18.4	How to Ask Questions	180
18.5	How to Aim Questions	182
18.6	Answering Questions	183

19 HOW TO TAKE ADVANTAGE OF THE INCREDIBLE POWER OF PRAISE — 185

19.1	What Do You Gain by Praising?	186
19.2	Why Don't We Praise	186
19.3	How to Praise in a Training Course	190
19.4	Guidelines on Praising in a Training Course	191

20 HOW TO MAXIMISE LEARNING BY TREATING LEARNERS AS APPRENTICES — 195

20.1	How Does Learning Process Work?	195
20.2	Stage 1: Deep Observation	196
20.3	Stage 2: Skill Acquisition	196
20.4	Stage 3: Experimentation	197
20.5	Why Repetition Is Fundamental to Learning	198
20.6	How Does This Apply to Training?	199

21 HOW TO HANDLE GROUP DYNAMICS AND CREATE EFFECTIVE LEARNING GROUPS — 203

21.1	How Groups Are Formed	204
21.2	How to Handle Group Issues	206
21.3	Effective Learning Groups	207

22 HOW TO RESPOND IF YOUR TRAINING OR IDEAS ARE CHALLENGED — 211

22.1	You Are Wrong, I Am Right!	211
22.2	How to Handle Criticism	212
22.3	What Not to Do When Challenged	214
22.4	Why People Might Be Already Thinking Negatively About the Course	214
22.5	How to Take a Pre-Emptive Approach	215

23 TRAINING SCENARIOS — 219

23.1	THE CASCADE EFFECT	219
23.2	WHAT MAKES A BAD TRAINING SESSION?	220
23.3	AVOID LECTURING	220
23.4	SHOW HOW IT IS DONE	222
23.5	ALLOW THINKING TIME	224
23.6	DO NOT RIDICULE	225
23.7	DON'T ASK CLOSED QUESTIONS	227
23.8	IMMERSE THE DELEGATES INTO THE TOPIC USING ALL THEIR SENSES	229
23.9	DESCRIBE WHY SOMETHING SHOULD BE LEARNED	230
23.10	CREATE A COMFORTABLE LEARNING ATMOSPHERE	232
23.11	START THE COURSE SMOOTHLY	233
23.12	SET A CLEAR OBJECTIVE	234
23.13	LEARNERS SHOULD LEARN ON THEIR OWN	235
23.14	RELATE TO THE LEARNER'S WORLD	237
23.15	USE COLLABORATION	238
23.16	USE MANY EXAMPLES	239
23.17	USE MNEMONICS TO HELP LEARNERS REMEMBER SEQUENCES	241
23.18	USE POSITIVE ENCOURAGEMENT	242
23.19	DON'T GIVE GENERIC FEEDBACK	243
23.20	DON'T CRITICISE HARSHLY	245
23.21	USE BALANCED DISCUSSIONS	247
23.22	HELP PEOPLE TO LEARN FROM EACH OTHER	248
23.23	GIVE MEANINGFUL HANDOUTS	250
23.24	BE ORGANISED	251
23.25	BEWARE OF TECHNOLOGY	252
23.26	EXPAND SLIDES FURTHER THAN WHAT APPEARS IN THEM	255
23.27	BE CONSISTENT ON WHAT YOU COVER	256
23.28	MAKE THE TRAINING EXCITING	257
23.29	MAKE SLIDES EXCITING	259
23.30	MAKE THE SLIDES INFORMATIVE	260
23.31	GET DELEGATES TO MOVE AROUND	262
23.32	TEST THEIR KNOWLEDGE	263
23.33	DELIVER FOCUSED TRAINING	264
23.34	DO NOT CUT OFF INTERESTING CONVERSATIONS	266
23.35	MINIMISE VISUAL DISTRACTIONS	267
23.36	MIX UP THE GROUPS	268
23.37	BEWARE OF TALKATIVE DELEGATES	269
23.38	PRESENT TO DELEGATES NOT TO THE SCREEN	271
23.39	MANAGE CONVERSATIONS	272
23.40	INVOLVE RATHER THAN DICTATE	274

Train the Trainer: The Art of Training Delivery

23.41	BE ENGAGING AND ANIMATED	275
23.42	MANAGE YOUR STRESS BY BEING PREPARED	276
23.43	GET THE TIMING OF YOUR COURSE RIGHT	278
23.44	CONSIDER YOUR DELEGATES' STATE OF MIND	280
23.45	MANAGE BREAK TIMES PRECISELY	281
23.46	END THE COURSE GRACEFULLY	282
23.47	COLLECT FEEDBACK IN A WAY THAT REFLECTS TRUE OPINION	284

24 FINAL REMARKS — 289

APPENDIX A: TRAINING PLAN MATRIX — 291

APPENDIX B: ACTION PLAN — 295

APPENDIX C: SOLUTIONS FOR HOMEWORK — 299

APPENDIX D: RECOMMENDED READING — 301

REFERENCES — 303

INDEX — 307

Skills Converged

Foreword

"In all my affairs it's a healthy thing now and then to hang a question mark on the things you have long taken for granted."

Bertrand Russell

We have all attended training courses that we thought could have been much better conducted and more useful. We have also attended courses that were so good we could not get enough. What distinguishes the two? How come some trainers are so good at this art? Do we expect our trainers to be the world's most prominent experts on a given topic? Probably not. They are certainly experts in their domains, but what usually makes them great trainers is their training methodology, enthusiasm for the domain and love of teaching. To train people on a given subject you need to be good at two things; the *domain* and *training people*.

The problem is that most trainers are good at the domain part but not so good at the training part. The reason is perhaps to do with what domain experts think of training. They go through school and university. They attend numerous lectures until they become domain experts. Naturally, they come to think that the way they were taught is the way to teach others too. Once they become an expert in something and decide to start training others, most trainers tend to fall back to the same methods used to teach them. This is where the problem starts; most trainers utilise teaching methods that were used in schools and universities that they are familiar with. They then apply these methods in their own training courses. Methods used in schools are generally suitable for a much younger crowed who need a lot more information than analysis and application because they don't know much about anything. Hence, teaching methods tend to be mainly one way. With universities, the aim is to teach many people at once. It is teaching on an industrial scale and hence it is not customised to the students' needs. University teaching is geared towards preparing students to get a job in business or academia.

Training courses are different. People are already skilled in many areas but are looking either to enhance one skill further or to add more skills to their arsenal. For them, application of a skill is crucial. Unlike university students, delegates in training courses are more time-conscious than resource-conscious. They want results that can lead to something tangible—monetary or otherwise. They want these results to last and they want change. Because of this, it is crucial to treat training differently. The ability to train others is a skill that is immensely useful and can be used in whatever domain you are good at. Hence, it is a skill for life and worth mastering.

This book will cover all the important areas of training people. Your domain could be technical, soft skills or even art related. Once you know the secret to conducting a good training session you can confidently use your expertise and domain knowledge in your training courses.

Much has been researched and discovered in the past several decades in the training industry but many of these findings have not been put to good use. In this book, you will be introduced to the most effective strategies and techniques discovered so far within the field of education, learning and training. By using the teachings of this book, you will become an impeccable trainer.

The focus of the book is mainly on delivery of training content rather than designing content. Instead of authoring your own content you can easily obtain professionally made training materials to save time and effort. At Skills Converged we provide various training materials on soft skills, management and productivity designed in line with fundamental principles of providing useful and long-lasting training. For best results, use this guide in conjunction with the training materials obtained from Skills Converged to deliver state of the art training course for your clients.

Dr. Ethan Honary
Founder
Skills Converged Ltd.

1 What Can You Learn from Awful Training Courses?

You are attending a course to learn how to operate a factory machine that helps cutting plastic into various shapes. The trainer starts by giving basic instructions on how to use the display and the buttons next to it to operate the complex machine. He goes on like this, "Look, it's really simple. You press A, the display shows 'ready'. Then you place the plastic block here. Never ever put your hand here. Insert it like this. Ok let me see." He then punches a bunch of buttons in sequence without explaining anything. "Ok, now we are ready to go. Now press B and bang! Haha, it is cutting. You know this machine is so fancy. You guys are so lucky. Years ago, we had to do all the cutting by hand, we had these sharpening tools that took forever to use. Tony, do you remember? Now this machine makes it too easy, if you know how to use it. Tony, do you remember when Ali was here, such a funny guy... We used to make all sorts of shapes back then. You don't want know some of the stuff we were making...One day we made..."

After a few more minutes of story telling the trainer says, "Ok, so who wants to have a go? Agnes you go first." Agnes is expecting a little help as she is not quite sure what to do. "Why are you looking at me? Just do what I told you." Agnes proceeds to press A on the display at which point the trainer almost shouts, "What do you think you are doing?!" Agnes is frozen in shock, "That's what you said we should do." The trainer says, "Did you remove the shaped block. No. You must remove the block first before pressing A. Ok, let

Train the Trainer: The Art of Training Delivery

me remove it for you. Now carry on. I cannot believe you did that!" Agnes is now visibly nervous. She doesn't want to make another mistake. She is so nervous she cannot remember the next step. So she just stares at the display.

The trainer is impatient, "Ok, you don't know the next step either!" He sighs, "Watch and learn." He then proceeds to select a few menu options on the display without explaining, "Got that? It's not that hard. So what do you do next?" Agnes says rather slowly, "I press B?" The trainer says, "Don't look at me. I am not saying anything." Agnes then proceeds slowly and presses B. The trainer jumps and presses the stop button and shouts, "Why on earth did you do that. Didn't you forget something? The raw block maybe? You need to put the new block in before pressing B. Man! You get 3 out of 10 for that performance, if that. I think I have a list of areas you need to develop. Ok. Who wants to try next?" Nobody volunteers.

Let's call this Example A and look at another example.

All delegates are present and ready for a course on Self-Assessment and Tax Calculations which is provided by the local council in the city. However, there is no sign of the trainer. The course is supposed to start at 9:00am. At 9:05, the trainer finally enters the room with a few sheets of paper in her hands. She says hi to everyone and explains that she had to make some copies and that is why she is late.

She hurries over to her desk and starts searching through her pile of papers. She seems to be looking for something that is necessary to start the course. Everyone is watching her in silence. After a whole minute she still has not found what she is looking for. She sighs and decides to skip this but is clearly irritated by the misplacement.

The trainer starts the training course by showing a slide on the projector's screen. She then goes straight through the title slide and then moves to the next slide while reading from it. She continues lecturing the delegates for the next 20 minutes, constantly talking. During this time none of the delegates have said a single word.

Let's call this Example B. Now let's look at one final example.

You are a delegate attending a course on Project Management. The trainer has provided a printout of the slides for you to use as a reference. The slides are full of text and very difficult to follow on the screen. There is just a lot of text to read when looking at the slides but not enough when reading them from the printout of the slides.

Just before explaining the maths behind the risk calculations, the trainer says, "I am sorry that you have to go through this. I know it is boring, but I have to cover it."

During the explanation, delegates don't seem to be paying much attention and are not really looking at the trainer. Everyone looks bored.

The trainer occasionally asks some questions. Before delegates have a chance to think more and reply, the trainer continues by providing the answer to his own question. Delegates remain quiet during subsequent questions.

The training course eventually becomes a one-way lecture with a bored audience that don't seem to be interested in the course.

Let's call this Example C.

1.1 What Is This Book About?

Surely, no trainer wants to end up training people like the above three examples. There is a method to the art of training and this book aims to share this method with you.

You will be introduced to a series of hands-on best practice guidelines on improving your training delivery. If you are a trainer, you already know how important it is to periodically review critical skills and expand your knowledge in important areas such as training methodology.

If you are new to training, it pays to study the field first and use established methods. This means that you don't have to spend your precious time to discover the best methods by trial and error.

So whether you are a freelance trainer, a trainer working for a training organisation or an expert in a particular field who wants to break into the training industry, this book is for you.

Throughout the book, you will go through case studies and guidelines on how to handle difficult situations. You learn about poor examples of training delivery and how to setup your training environment so that everything works for you rather than against you. The book guides you to achieve a single critical goal—how to maximise learning that lasts.

1.2 What You Should Promise to Do

Now, we need to be honest with you. To get the most from this book you need to spend time and work on your skills. As the saying is, there is no free lunch; no pain no gain. Considering how much you can benefit from delivering an effective training, the time invested in mastering the skills is insignificant. Effective training delivery will lead to increased fame and fortune as more people want to be trained by you.

The book is designed as a self-study course so that you can go through a number of exercises to reflect on your own performance and draw up an action plan. We cannot stress enough the importance of follow-through after you have read each chapter. Each chapter is followed by specific homework. Consider spending at least an hour on each homework and reflect on the content of the chapter before moving on to the next chapter.

You can also consider discussing the lessons learned from the book in the dedicated Linked-In Group[1] for this book with other fellow members of the training community for further insights into the art of training.

1.3 Terminology: Who Are Delegates?

In this book, we often refer to people who attend a training course as *delegates*. We use this word for consistency, though various other terms can and might be used. These are *trainee*, *student*, *learner* or *participant*. In the context of training, they all mean the same.

1.4 Terminology: What Kind of Training?

The focus of this book is to cover best practice guidelines for an interactive training environment.

In this setting, a combination of instructional methods can be used to train delegates. Unfortunately, many think that you either should focus on lecturing or get the delegates to have a discussion on a topic. You will see that with most courses a combined approach is the most effective.

Study the list of instructional methods[2] to learn about each technique. It is important to be aware of the existence of each method in order to employ it. If you are using ready-made training materials, the course designer would have already decided on which method to use and at what point in the course, so you only need to follow through with the appropriate method.

---

[1] www.linkedin.com/groups/12279712/

[2] www.skillsconverged.com/TraintheTrainer/LearntoTeach/InstructionalMethods.aspx

1.5 How to Avoid Poor Training Delivery

Let's go back to the examples provided at the beginning of this chapter.

In Example A, the trainer has several shortcomings. The way he is giving instructions is poor. He doesn't describe every step, or review the sequence of steps but expects everyone to memorise it straight away. He doesn't ask or check delegates' knowledge to make sure trainees understand what he is talking about. He then gets side tracked with an irrelevant story which is highly distracting and adds more problems. By the time he finishes his story, some trainees have forgotten the sequence of instructions. This is not their fault; it is the trainer's fault.

When he asks for a volunteer, the trainer seems intent to use the volunteer and her mistakes to teach others what not to do. It is as if the trainer is waiting and hoping for the volunteer to make mistakes so he can make a point out of it. His feedback and remarks are sarcastic at best and somewhat rude. The overall effect is that his remarks reduce the trainee's confidence in her own abilities and make her doubt whatever details she could remember. Indeed, the experience will be traumatic for her. The problem is that the trainer thinks his training has been successful. He has managed to teach the delegates by getting them to observe mistakes. He has made a scene so that they can remember what he has told them.

Unfortunately, such attitude and mannerism will be detrimental to any learning, be it for Agnes who has been put on the spot, or others. Amazingly, this style of 'tough' teaching seems to be quite common. Some trainers think that the tougher they are, the more people learn. They think it doesn't matter how they express this toughness; so long as the delegates are in fear of them, all is fine. Even if this approach worked (for about a second and a half), it would be for all the wrong reasons and should be avoided entirely. In this book, you will learn about the right mentality and approach. You will learn how to avoid such damaging practices and instead use systematic training methodologies that boost learning significantly.

In Example B, the trainer is disorganised. This can create a bad first impression. A poor start at the beginning of the training course means that you need to work really hard for the rest of it to gain back the audience's confidence in your training ability. Once people doubt your expertise or ability to train, it becomes very difficult for them to learn anything from you. They simply dismiss what you say, don't pay attention and may start to think that attending the course was a waste of time.

The objective of a training course is to maximise learning on a particular subject. Countless studies show that this can happen when learners are involved. A passive listening-only approach does little more than raising awareness of the subject. If you want to teach, you need interaction.

The question is; what is interaction? Is filling a questionnaire an interaction? Not really. Is answering multiple-choice questions in an e-learning course an interaction? Again, the answer is no. In this book, you will learn about the fundamental principles of learning through interactions.

In Example C, the trainer undermines himself before he even explains a topic. This is basically a poor training style. This style is irrespective of his expertise or the interactivity of the content. In the same example, the trainer keeps answering his own questions, thereby, inadvertently 'teaching' the delegates not to reply to his questions. This book also aims to address such issues in addition to gains achieved using the right kind of training methodology.

Throughout the book we refer to a variety of resources such as exercises or icebreakers available for free on our website SkillsConverged.com. Simply search for the title given here and you can easily find the full instructions on the website.

In the next chapter, you will learn what it takes to become a great trainer. You will learn that by adopting one fundamental mindset you can significantly improve the quality of your training and differentiate yourself from those who are not aware of this mindset. But before moving on, there is some homework for you to complete.

Homework

1. Recall two training courses you have attended in the past, as a delegate, that you were positively impressed with. This can be any course such as a language course, a technical course, hobbies, art courses, etc. Why did you like them? What was impressive about them?

2. Recall two training courses that you did not enjoy or thought that were poorly delivered. What went wrong? Was it the content or the delivery that let you down?

3. Now, analyse the examples by looking for patterns. Do you see similarities between training courses that went well? What makes them successful?

4. What is similar about the less effective courses? What can you do to avoid this kind of poor performance?

2 What Does It Take to Become a Great Trainer?

In this chapter, you will learn how to become an exceptional trainer. Why is it that some training courses are effective, memorable and loved by delegates while others are boring, ineffective and easily forgotten?

There are many techniques and methods proposed over the years that claim to be the most effective training method yet. However, rather than jumping ahead to use a specific method and expecting immediate results, it pays to know what's wrong with bad training first. From this you can see what works in principle and what doesn't. This mindset will help on many fronts. It helps you to choose the right techniques and also to know what can be compromised in case of an emergency.

The best way to improve your training effectiveness is to have the correct mindset when training others which is the objective of this chapter. Everything else can then follow the core principles.

2.1 Why a Trainer's Expertise Can Be a Turn Off

Let's look at an example. Consider a trainer who is teaching Project Management. He has been managing projects for years but has not been involved in training people on the topic. Since he is an expert in this field, he likes to share his expertise and experiences. Throughout the course he seizes every opportunity to relate back to a great piece of work he has done in the past and how *he* did it in a magnificent way. The delegates in his class might learn some aspects of his methods, but will increasingly feel overwhelmed, or even irritated by the constant self-promotion and self-gratification.

It is quite possible that the trainer is not an arrogant person and is not trying to show off. He might think that as an expert in the subject he is helping his delegates by sharing his wisdom. The delegates on the other hand see this as boasting and can be put off by it.

The problem with many training courses that don't work is that a trainer thinks the success of the training course depends solely on *their* expertise and *their* performance in delivering this expertise. This is a *trainer centred* approach. Unfortunately, it does not lead to an effective training course simply because the learners are ignored. Their needs, their background and their participation are considered secondary to the trainer's expertise and experience.

This mentality leads to one-directional courses that people often find boring and useless. Participants usually don't know why they have to learn something and are sometimes de-motivated by being constantly reminded that their teacher knows a lot more about the subject than they could possibly ever learn.

2.2 What Should Training Be Centred On?

You may wonder what the right approach is. Training is fundamentally about *facilitation*; facilitating the process of learning and the exchange of information.

2.2 What Should Training Be Centred On?

> If you are going to train others on any topic, first and foremost, you should consider yourself a *facilitating trainer*. This will then help you to align everything you do with your core objective.

This philosophy has certain implications. It means that you no longer have to view yourself as the source of all information. Instead, you look for opportunities to maximise learning, as you would do if you think of yourself as the facilitator of this process.

This simple mentality leads to the following contrast between a facilitating trainer and a trainer who is focused on showcasing his own expertise. Let's call this second trainer, a *lecturing trainer*:

- A facilitating trainer encourages trainees to learn from each other as well as from the trainer.
- A facilitating trainer understands the value of trainees' participation in the learning process.
- A facilitating trainer will not rush to answer a question. Instead, he uses this as an opportunity to engage all trainees, to make them think about the issues more extensively using their current understanding and to subsequently help them learn more in the process.
- A facilitating trainer will praise trainees for learning rather than see their knowledge as a competition to his own. A facilitating trainer will become increasingly satisfied as learners learn more. A trainer who is focused on showcasing his own expertise (a lecturing trainer) will feel progressively intimidated as trainees challenge his views or learn about a subject faster than the trainer has done in the past.
- A facilitating trainer will be interested to know how much trainees know about the subject and works hard to increase their knowledge. In contrast, a lecturing trainer only wants to lecture the trainees. This is irrespective of what they know, what they like to know and the pace at which they want to learn the new material.
- A facilitating trainer is happy to accept the limitation of his knowledge. A lecturing trainer is inclined to fake his expertise when challenged and might feel threatened when asked about subjects that he doesn't know much about.
- A facilitating trainer sees himself as a learner too and considers each training course as a learning opportunity to improve his own

knowledge. He can then provide a better training next time around. A lecturing trainer sees the training course as a one-way communication channel; from him to others. For him, the training course is a mechanism to *advertise* his talents.

In short, a facilitating trainer understands that learning takes place through a cross-pollination of ideas within a group including him, and his role is to maximise this exchange of information.

However, be careful not to become only a facilitator. Foremost, you are a trainer. A facilitator serves people when they need help, usually in terms of access to information or needing clarifications on procedures. As a facilitating trainer you must add a lot more to this. You must understand what your delegates need at any given point. You must know what is important for them to learn and at what pace they should learn it. You are effectively leading them as opposed to just reacting to them which is usually what a facilitator does. Aim to be both a trainer and a facilitator.

2.3 Key Principles in Adult Learning

Many academics in the field of educational psychology believe that the following conditions must be true for people to learn more effectively:

- *Must be safe.* The learning environment must be welcoming and safe.
- *Must be active.* A learner should be an active participant in the learning process.
- *Have a clear need.* Learners must feel that they need to learn the subject matter.
- *Be socially comfortable.* The learning environment must be socially comfortable.
- *Be physically comfortable.* The learning environment must also be physically optimised with good lighting, ventilation, size and efficient table and chair configuration. There will be a detailed guide on this topic in later chapters.
- *Be two-way.* Learning must be based on a two-way communication channel.
- *Have own goals.* Learners must set their own learning goals.
- *Make evaluations.* Learners should be able to evaluate their own progress and clearly see that the training has been successful.
- *Relate the subject.* Learners should be able to relate the subject matter to their own previous experience and build on it to take it to the next level.

To become a great trainer, you need to have a mindset that is focused entirely on learners. This mindset opens up multitudes of techniques that can be used to maximise learning efficiency.

Homework

Use the following form to evaluate your current training performance. Use copies of this form in your courses to analyse them. Keep a copy of the filled-in form so you can come back to see how you can apply various lessons learned in the book to improve different aspects of your training.

Pick one of your typical training courses. Answer the following questions about this course. State the facts or answer by yes or no and expand with one or two sentences. Be honest with yourself—no one else is going to read your evaluation. Use it as an opportunity to spot areas that you need to work on more.

Name of the course:
1. How many training exercises do you have in your course?
2. How long is the longest training exercise in this course?
3. How much of the time you spend in the course is used by you to lecture and *give* information as opposed to allowing delegates to express their opinion and participate in discussions and exercises. Provide a percentage.
4. Do you tend to answer delegates' questions directly and promptly or are you more likely to reflect it back to trainees when you see an opportunity to get them to learn something new?

5. Do you ever feel threatened when delegates ask you a question that you don't know the answers to? How do you usually handle these questions?

6. How often do you praise your delegates for providing answers or insights to topics?

7. How often do you change your training course content? Do you update it after every delivery based on what you have learned from your experience or do you tend to stick to what you already have?

8. Considering what you have learned about the difference between a facilitator and a lecturing trainer, where would you place yourself between the two styles? Mark an X on the spectrum.

Facilitating Trainer ◄─────────┼─────────► Lecturing Trainer

3 What Is Accelerated Learning?

You might have heard of Accelerated Learning (AL) and wonder what it is all about. Why is it considered so effective? Where does it come from? How do we know that it works? Who is it for? Most importantly, can you employ it in your training courses to get the best from your training sessions?

Accelerated Learning is a system designed to maximise learning. It is not necessarily a specific method; instead, it is a series of guidelines and methodologies that help increase the efficiency of learning. The aim is simple; you want to increase knowledge transfer and knowledge retention while spending the least amount of time in the process. The efficiency leads to reduced costs and the total time it takes to teach something to people with long lasting results.

This goal is rather grand which is perhaps why AL has gained so much attention in the past few decades. The good news is that AL works and numerous studies support the underlying principles and methodologies used.

Accelerated Learning, in its most fundamental level, is based on how we naturally learn. The aim is to involve all senses of a learner rather than just relying on a few. The learner will be physically and psychologically immersed in the learning task and therefor learn much faster. For example, images, colours, sounds, music, physical activity and the environment are used in an orchestrated way to accelerate learning.

Before moving on to methodology, let's look at the history and early development of AL.

3.1 The History

In 1970s, the Bulgarian psychotherapist Geori Lozanov developed a teaching method known as *suggestopedia* (Lozanov 1970). It is used mainly to teach foreign languages. With this methodology the physical surroundings are set in such a way to help the students feel comfortable and confident to learn. Here are some of the activities carried out for teaching a language:

- *Teaching is playful.* The teacher introduces new concepts in a playful manner, rather than the traditional boring style of focusing on grammar and lexicon.
- *There is background music.* Music is played in the background while a text is read by the teacher at normal speed. The type of music is usually baroque.
- *Students follow the teacher.* The teacher reads the text and sometimes intones some of the words. Students are supposed to follow suit.
- *Students elaborate.* During the elaboration phase, students go through a number of games, drama roleplays and songs to practice some more.
- *Production stage tests students.* During this phase, students speak the language without interruption or being corrected by the teacher.

Lozanov's work opened up the field and showed the scientific community that learning methodology can be enhanced by following a number of rather simple principles.

In 1980s, Howard Gardner published his important book, *"Frames of Mind: The Theory of Multiple Intelligences"* which had a significant effect on our understanding of intelligence (Gardner 1993). The principle was that intelligence was not just a single general ability and that instead there were "modalities" catering for specific sensory inputs. Gardner suggested eight primary abilities, or intelligences:

- Musical-rhythmic
- Verbal-linguistic
- Visual-spatial
- Logical-mathematical
- Kinesthetic
- Interpersonal
- Intrapersonal
- Naturalistic

It is important to note that the idea of multiple intelligences is not to cast or label an individual into a specific category. Instead, rather than restricting them into a specific modality, the aim is to empower each person through all modalities. In other words, there is more to intelligence than just being good at logic and math.

Perhaps we should go back to examine the motivation for proposing such a theory. At the time, IQ tests were all the rage. It seemed that all you needed to do to examine the intelligence capability of a student was to get them go through an IQ test and see how much they scored. Gardner saw a problem with this that the IQ tests generally measured people for their logic and mathematical intelligence and left out a whole lot of other areas, or modalities that an individual can perform in and be good at. Hence, Gardner's theory suggests that students are better served when a teacher uses methodologies, exercises and activities that cater for all students rather than only those who have a stronger logical or linguistic intelligences.

Gardner's research led to a great breakthrough in understanding why some students failed so badly in traditional schools. To take advantage of multiple intelligences while teaching, Gardner summarises his approach for teachers as follows:

- *Individualise the teaching.* Personalise your teaching style to suit the most effective method for each learner.
- *Pluralize the teaching.* Consider teaching important lessons and materials in multiple ways. Sometimes you may not know in advance which modality each learner is strong at. By teaching in multiple ways, you maximise the chances that all students learn the topics rather than just a few who matched your teaching method.

In 1985, Colin Rose published, *"Accelerated Learning"* which was the first popular book on the topic (Rose 1985). The book expanded on the research by Lozanov and other recent research on learning methodologies. In 1996, this was followed by Alistair Smith's book, *"Accelerated Learning in the Classroom."* (Smith 1996) This then became a standard book in the UK and it is an important one to read to understand AL on a deeper level. This led to an increase in the number of books published in this area such as anther useful book, *"The Accelerated Learning Handbook"* by Dave Meier (Meier 2000).

Now let's see what accelerated learning is all about.

3.2 The Setup of the Environment

There are two aspects to consider; one is to set up the right environment and the other to follow a set process that helps learners learn faster. To create an optimal learning environment, consider the following:

- *Create an ideal physical environment for learning.* Learners learn most effectively when in the right physical environment. The environment should have fresh air, adequate light, comfortable temperature levels and with minimal noise or visual distractions. Learners should be well-fed and hydrated. The key is to focus on physical needs. If they have been sitting for an hour, they are bound to start feeling uncomfortable or need to stretch their legs. Pushing ahead with teaching when you can see that learners are fidgeting or shifting a lot is just wrong. It may mean you need to take an earlier break despite your schedule, otherwise you may risk wasting your time by trying to continue with teaching.
- *Create an ideal psychological environment for learning.* Emotional stress is a strong barrier to learning. Learners need to be motivated which means that first and foremost, they need to know why they are supposed to learn something. This is particularly important for adult learners. If not convinced, they will not engage and may even become actively resistant to participate. Equally, it is important to have a positive learning environment. Learners must feel safe and cared for rather than being forced to learn for fear of punishment, humiliation and ridicule whether directly or indirectly.
- *Create collaboration among learners.* Learners learn greatly from each other. Traditional methods create a competitive environment where learners are encouraged to hold information away from other learners hoping to stand out, get a higher score and eventually get a preferential treatment. With AL, the aim is to focus on collaborative learning. AL sessions contain numerous group exercises where learners work together to solve problems, support each other and work together towards a common goal.
- *Involve learners totally.* People learn best when they are totally immersed in a topic and feel fully responsible for the learning task. Learning is not a passive activity; it is active and fully involved. This is precisely why so many training attempts fail since they are provided in the style of a presentation or lecture. There is very little intake in such situations and retention is very low because learners are not actively involved. AL, in contrast, is based heavily on exercises and active involvement.

- *Use variety in your teaching to appeal to all intelligences.* In line with the multiple intelligences theory, you must use a variety of teaching methods to deliver the content. Learning activities must be designed around several modalities and sensory stimulus taking into account different intelligences and possibly learning styles.
- *Use contextual learning.* People learn better in context. A context helps with memory and retention. By getting involved in a realistic scenario, learners can see exactly what needs to be done to accomplish a task. For example, to explain how to operate a machine, you can get the learners to actually interact with the machine while you teach them. This is learning in context rather than explaining the operation verbally in a classroom and expect them to know what to do a few days later when they are standing in front of the machine.
- *Aim for results.* The ultimate aim of AL is to get long lasting results and to get them fast. Whatever method helps you achieve this is worth considering. As technology evolves, new techniques can be incorporated into the AL methodology to help with the process. As such AL is not cast in stone; instead, it is ultimately about maximisation of learning by any suitable methods.

> By definition, AL is about creating an environment and using methods that can accelerate the learning process. The objective is to enhance the results and not necessarily to use specific methods. AL is results-oriented, it is the end that matters, not the means. In other words, any method that can help you increase the speed of learning and quality of retention, by definition, falls under Accelerated Learning.

3.3 The Guiding Principles

In line with setting up the right environment, you must also consider the following guiding principles:

- *Learning comes from doing the actual work.* Learners must be involved and there must be a feedback loop present so that actions can be corrected. This feedback loop is critical. Without it learners won't know how to improve their skills.

- ***Learning is about creating rather than consuming***. New knowledge cannot be retained for long or understood fully unless it is related and integrated with the rest of the learner's knowledge. This active creation phase is essential in correctly learning something new. Without the active creation, it will be memorisation of raw data that won't be retained for long.
- ***All senses are involved***. Vision is our strongest sense. An image seen is remembered much easier than a sentence heard. In a series of experiments, 1000 photos were shown to people at a pace of one per second. The experimenters mixed another 100 photos with the original 1000 and asked the participants to select those they had not seen the first time. Amazingly, everyone was able to identify which photos they had seen previously and which they had not (Buzan 2009). Further studies in this area are even more amazing. They show that if an individual is shown 100,000 images, he can still tell, with about 97% accuracy, if a sample image was part of that set. Using a rich set of images, videos, illustrations, diagrams and the like can significantly enhance learning. Activities must be designed in a way to exploit all senses and maximise information transfer. For example, using carefully chosen music in the background can help learners associate a given topic with a given sound thereby helping their memory and recall.
- ***Learning should take place in a positive environment***. Praise the delegates often. To praise, you will need to observe learners while engaged in activities. A passive method not only leads to boredom and disengagement, but also deprives you the opportunity to praise your delegates.
- ***Group work enhances learning***. Cooperative exercises create a positive atmosphere for learning and also help with learning and remembering the shared experience afterwards.
- ***Provide adequate breaks***. People are not superhuman. There is only so much they can take in. Teaching a tired brain is a waste of time. Accelerated learning is not about accelerating through content at all costs. It is about maximising retention with minimal effort.
- ***Encourage learners to set personal goals***. Self-analysis coupled with a specific goal is a great motivator. It also helps learners to know where they need to focus on and how close they are to reach their personal goal.
- ***Provide loving support***. Imagine when a child is just learning how to ride a bike. A caring parent explains and guides the child but eventually the support becomes unnoticeable. The child cannot tell if the parent is still holding the bike. The parent, however, is ready to

intervene and support the child but needs to "let go" so the child eventually learns to stabilise the bike and pedal ahead. There is strong *love, trust* and *patience* in this exchange. In the same way, learners under an accelerated learning system might be unaware of the support given to them by the trainer. However, they *trust* the trainer and follow the *guidance* knowing that if they *persist* they will eventually learn the skills. As a trainer, your passion and care will support them to push through any challenges.
- *Providing freedom.* Freedom allows a student to feel that he is in control of the learning. With freedom you can allow students to participate in certain exercises if it matches their disposition. The class is no longer a rigid and boring formal place. Instead, a student is free to move or leave the class so long as he or she not disrupting others. This creates a level of trust between the students and the trainer that in conjunction with love, care and passion for the topic can be quite empowering.

3.4 Accelerated Learning Techniques

Now that you have learned about the underlying principles and the overall structure of AL, you may wonder what you can do as a trainer to take advantage of this methodology. Here is a handy list of actions you can take to apply AL:

- *Place the learner in the right environment.* Design an ideal physical and psychological environment as explained earlier.
- *Make learners feel comfortable with each other.* Use icebreakers. Choose one that is suitable for the age group of delegates or one that matches their background and industry. A large library of free icebreakers is provided at SkillsConverged.com.
- *Explain the background and theory of a given topic.* Ask questions and expect answers to make sure learners remain engaged.
- *Follow theory with an exercise to get learners practice the skills.* Use carefully designed exercises that help learners practice what they were just taught. The exercises must be engaging, entertaining and precise so focus is maintained.
- *Set clear objectives.* Demonstrate that learners have achieved the objectives at the end of each session.
- *Ask questions.* Create curiosity. Engage the learners' minds by asking them questions rather than telling them. The questions should be formulated to guide learners about the topic you have in mind. Think of yourself as a wise man with an apprentice. You don't have to tell the apprentice everything in detail—sometimes the apprentice needs

to find out for himself. This self-discovery can lead to learning that lasts much longer than if you just told them about the topic. Guided questions help you achieve this.
- *Get learners to answer "What's in it for me?"* Learning can be significantly boosted when a learner knows why he needs to learn something. By spending enough time on answering this question you can minimise the risk of disengagement later when you get to tougher parts of a subject that requires concentration and effort.
- *Get learners to describe what they have learned in their own words*. Get them to paraphrase aloud. Verbalisation exposes areas that are not learned well so a student can immediately improve those weak points. Describing aloud also creates another opportunity for multi-sensory learning.
- *Use chunking to help memorisation of key concepts*. Divide the content into chunks and sessions to make absorption easier.
- *Get them to illustrate the concept or draw a mind map*. Visualisation of a concept can significantly help with memory, understanding and retention. Techniques such as mind mapping are known to be extremely effective in this regard. To get the most, divide the learners into groups and ask them to work together to create a visual representation of what they have learned. The collaboration, along with the visual content will significantly accelerate the learning process.
- *Involve other senses*. Use activities that involve touch, sound and visuals. Use taste and smell too. The sensory stimulus can act as a trigger for recall later on. Rich sensory experiences also help to make the activity more unique and in turn easier to recall. For example, ask learners to sort some cards into a particular ranking order while working together. This will involve touch, sound and vision.
- *Test learner's knowledge*. Don't keep jumping from one subject to the next. Pause to make sure that what you have covered has sunk in and that everyone is clear about it. Learners learn at different rates and considering that people have multiple intelligences, they also respond in different ways. A pause is necessary to help everybody catch up before you move on to the next topic. A test in the form of an exercise encourages critical thinking, recall and a deeper understanding of the topic.
- *Get learners to move physically*. Periodically go through exercises that require delegates to move. Gather learners in pairs or groups of three or use exercises that require direct movement such as passing a ball. Make sure the physical movement does not become too much of a distraction though.

- *Get learners to visualise themselves as experts.* Part of becoming skilled in something is to visualise how you are when you have the skill. This can significantly help an individual to use immersive learning and see themselves achieving the goal. It also helps to set a precise goal to aim for.
- *Get learners to teach another person on what they have learned.* This is rather easy for self-learning and very effective. Once you learn something, try explaining it to others and your understanding of the topic will increase significantly. To apply it to learners in a class, this requires more planning. You will need to use exercises that put learners together and select one to teach the other and vice versa. Shared problem solving can help with this approach as well. You can also do this sequentially. Teach one subject to one group and another subject to another group. Ask each group to teach the other group about the topic they have just learned about.
- *Get learners to go through elaborate exercises.* Get delegates to play with colourful props, toys, cards and participate in cooperative or competitive games requiring plenty of movement. The experience becomes memorable and lessons can be taught much more effectively when learners get a chance to practice it on the spot rather than just listening to some theory. The cost is that you need to design and prepare for these exercises in advance. Fortunately, you can take advantage of our extensive library of such exercises to get a head start.
- *Use emotional display.* Emotions can act as a catalyst and make the content much more memorable. For example, in language teaching pictures with strong emotional value are used to teach vocabulary. Pictures with emotional content are more likely to be remembered and hence the association with the newly learned word can be stronger.
- *Teach by telling stories.* People love to hear stories. There is not a day that passes without us being exposed to some kind of a story, whether we hear about it on TV or from a friend or family. We don't seem to get tired of them. Stories with emotional content are easy to remember and can be used as an analogy or allegory. By including learners in a carefully structured story you can teach many concepts at once and expect them to remember lessons for a long time to come.

Homework

Consider the courses you provide or plan to provide on your expert topics. Answer the following questions for each course.

Find three icebreakers for your training courses that help bring people together. Make note of them here.

In your last training courses, did you ask enough questions or were you more inclined to use a lecturing method to give information? Considering the benefits of asking questions and AL demonstrated in this chapter, what should you do differently in your next course?

How can you get delegates to answer "What's in it for me?" Describe your strategy on how you approach this.

In what way can you engage all the delegates' senses in your training course? Think of techniques such as using exercises, demos, field trips, simulations, games, apps and computer-based training.

What kinds of elaborate exercises can you get delegates to go through that are based on AL?

How can you increase the emotional content of the course or exercises so that the course becomes more memorable? What strategies would you consider?

What stories can you tell to maximise engagement and retention while making learning easier? Make a brief note of them here but use separate sheets to record the actual stories.

4 How to Plan Your Training

When it comes to providing a training course, preparation can be the difference between success and failure. If you have delivered a training course before, you know that you cannot just walk into the room and start the session. Preparation is everything.

In this lesson, you will learn about different aspects of preparation that can make your training a success. The problem in most cases is that many trainers underestimate the effect of poor preparation on the final outcome. The aim in this chapter is to help you identify areas of training that need preparation.

Before delivering a course, you need to plan and find out about the following areas. The more you know, the easier it is to plan:

4.1 Who Are Your Delegates?

For training to be effective, it must be targeted. This means you need to know who you are training. Are they all from the same organisation? Do they know each other? Do they have a common background? Do they have any common problems? Have they attended similar training courses before?

4.2 What Do the Delegates Need to Learn?

This can be linked to a *Training Needs Analysis* (TNA) to customise the course. A TNA is a systematic way to determine what people need and discover skill gaps. In line with the business strategy of the organisation, TNA aims to increase employee productivity and workflow. TNA is explored in more detail in the next chapter.

If you are running a public course, know your delegates and their respective industries so that you can tailor the course accordingly.

4.3 What Do the Delegates Already Know?

This is particularly important if you are running a course on technical skills. You will need to know how experienced your delegates are so they can be enrolled at the right level. It also allows you to skip over content they already know and focus on those areas that they want to know more about.

A great way to discover what delegates already know is to ask them to fill in a questionnaire before attending the course.

Another method is to give a pre-course activity which delegates need to complete and bring to the class. Delegates can then present their work during the training session. This has several benefits; it allows you to quickly evaluate how much each person knows and which areas they need to improve on. It is also a great way to increase interaction between delegates. They can provide feedback to each other and you can use the discussions to highlight strengths and weaknesses of different methods.

For example, we use this technique in a course on Presentation Skills by asking delegates to prepare a short presentation and present it at the beginning of the course. The trainer can assess the needs of each presenter based on the quality of each presentation delivered. During the course the trainer can easily link a key lesson to a particular performance and teach specifically using examples. This significantly increases the impact of the lessons and makes them very vivid in the minds of delegates.

4.4 How Many People Are You Training?

In an interactive training course, there can be a lot of discussions and exercises. As the number of delegates goes up, you will end up spending more and more time in each activity or discussion. If you have too many people, you will not be able to cover many topics in this manner. Having too many delegates will naturally force you to lecture as opposed to train and facilitate.

> Our experience at Skills Converged is that the ideal number of delegates is no less than 6 and no more than 12 with the sweet spot of 8.

You need to have enough people to create groups, to encourage meaningful discussions and to increase knowledge share. With more than 12 people the course slows down considerably. The main issue is that if you decide to address an individual's question or specific concern, you will have 11 people waiting and listening. If the topic does not concern them much (which becomes more likely the more people you have), they can get bored.

Most training agencies and even business clients want to squeeze as many people as they can into a single course for financial reasons. As a trainer, you must resist this pressure because if the training doesn't go well, it is your reputation and expertise that would be questioned.

4.5 Where Is the Venue?

The choice of the venue determines your approach to training. In general, you have three options:

1. Public course in your own organisation
2. In-house course in a client's premises
3. Public or custom course in a training agency's premises

In each case you need to customise the training for your specific training needs. You will be introduced to *training room configuration* in Chapter 8, learning how to set up the training environment.

4.6 What Are You Trying to Achieve?

To run a successful course, you need to know from the outset what you are trying to achieve. What is your main aim? Are you aiming to increase delegates' productivity by getting to review their bad habits? Are you interested to highlight certain inter-team communication issues? Are you preparing them for an upcoming extensive restructuring and change in their organisation? Do you want to make them proficient at using a particular software?

If there is one thing you want your delegates to learn in the course, what would that be?

In all cases, knowing your core objective throughout the course can help you filter out unnecessary content, focus the discussion on important topics and highlight relevant material as opportunities arise.

> Knowing what you want to achieve increases your presence of mind and allows you to deliver a focused and effective training.

4.7 What Resources Do You Need for the Training Course?

In line with setting up the environment, you need to decide what you need to run the course. Do you need papers, laptops, equipment, props…?

Being organised is also critical. The manner you use your resources is part of your training performance and will be seen and judged by your delegates.

Imagine if delegates see a disorganised trainer who is constantly searching for a missing "something." Imagine their reaction when they see a trainer who struggles to operate a projector, a laptop or a sound recording device.

> Practice using gadgets before the course and consider this part of the preparation required for your on-stage performance.

4.8 How Would You Evaluate the Training Session?

Once you know the training needs of your delegates and what you want to achieve, establish a way to evaluate if you have achieved it or not. Training evaluation is not a straight forward activity and there is an art to this. It highly depends on the subject domain. It is much easier to evaluate people on technical skills or on using software than it is to judge them on soft skills such as productivity or communication skills.

In either case, you can use post-course activities, questionnaires and written or oral evaluations to see how much delegates have improved as a result of attending the course.

For soft skills, methods such as 360 degrees analysis before and after the course to analyse the effect of training on team performance and communication are useful.

Consider using the following types of assessment:

- *Assessing skills*. Use performance tests. The trainee performs under real or simulated conditions.
- *Assessing knowledge*. Use oral or written tests. These can be fixed response (answering multiple-choice questions) or open responses where trainees provide answers with their own specific expressions.
- *Assessing attitudes*. Use direct observation or use questionnaires.

4.9 What Are the Homework or Post-Course Activities?

Post-course activities have several benefits:

- **Refresh memory**. It allows you to refresh the trainees' minds about the topics discussed in the course. Periodic refreshing can help to transfer the skills from short term memory to long term memory.
- **Turning it into a habit**. Research shows that repeating a skill or activity for about 20 days makes it into a habit. You can use this principle when giving post-course activities.
- **Assessing the effectiveness of training**. Trainees' success or failure in the post-course activity can indicate if the training was effective or not. This in turn will allow you to improve your course accordingly.

4.10 How to Evaluate Your Own Performance

In addition to evaluating trainees' performance, you also need to know if your training delivery was successful or not and if any changes are needed. For this, ask for feedback from your delegates. Consider the following techniques to obtain this feedback:

Ask Them Directly

At the end of the course ask delegates directly what they liked the most and what they didn't like about the course. Their honest answer can be very valuable as it will help you improve your next training session.

Use a Questionnaire

A common method is to provide an evaluation form at the end of the course such as those bundled with our training materials. If properly designed, these forms give you a good insight into what trainees think of your training.

There are three options:

- ***Delegates fill in the forms and give them back to you.***
    - ***Action:*** You can then pass this on to your training agency if you work with one or just evaluate them after the course.
    - ***Issue:*** Delegates may not be as honest as they like to be since they know that they will return the forms to you and you can see the feedback they have given straight away. This can influence their opinion especially if they are going to attend another one of your courses.
- ***The agency contacts the delegates.***
    - ***Actions.*** The agency contacts the delegates directly and asks them to provide feedback. This can be through paper, email, online, phone or an app.
    - ***Issue:*** Calling on the phone can be invasive and costly. Some people may not spend the time to fill an online form or reply to an email that they have received after the course.
- ***Delegates fill in the forms and give them to the agency.***
    - ***Action:*** They can fill in the forms after the course (on paper or online) and provide their honest view about the training course to your training agency (if you have one).
    - ***Issue:*** Many delegates don't fill in the forms after the course which means the opportunity to receive feedback is lost. Even if they do, they may have forgotten about specific issues and may just fill in the forms as a formality.

Is there a better way to handle this? Here are a couple of solutions that address these issues.

Solution 1:

Provide an envelope with the form at the end of the course and explain explicitly that the forms should be placed inside sealed envelopes which will then be passed to the agency directly. Since you no longer can see the forms directly, delegates are likely to be more honest about their feedback. Of course, you will receive the feedback from the agency anyway, but at least this process helps delegates to be more honest and removes any psychological barrier that might prevent them from giving their true opinion. In the long run this approach is more beneficial to the quality of your training.

Solution 2:

At the end of the course distribute a number of non-sticky post-it notes to all delegates. They can have as many as they want. Ask delegates to write suggestions about improving the course, the areas they want you to cover or anything they want to see improved. Ask them to write one idea on each note, fold them and then put them in the box placed next to the door as they leave. You can use a ballot box if you like and take it with you to your courses. This way, delegates will know that you will not know who has written the feedback and will be more willing to write their true opinion. You should even encourage them to do this because you are eager to improve your course. You can say that you strongly welcome positive or constructive feedback. So long as you receive them, it is fine with you! Most people like to help when they can and they will. This kind of direct and relevant feedback is priceless. Use it to increase your chances of delivering impeccable courses and to stand out from the competition.

Homework

Consider your most recent training course and answer the following questions.

Title of the Course:

1. Did you know anything about the delegates before attending the course?

2. Did you have an ideal number of delegates present in the course?

3. Did you know your single most important objective as you went through the course? What was it?

4. Were you happy with the venue and the training environment?

5. What was the result of delegates' assessments after the course?

6. Was the feedback collection method effective? Did you receive honest feedback?

7. Did you spot a pattern in the feedback received from your delegates? What does this suggest?

8. Are you happy with the above feedback? Having answered these questions, identify a number of actions that help you improve your training course preparation and list these actions below:

5 What Is Training Needs Analysis?

In this chapter, you will learn about Training Needs Analysis or its widely used acronym, TNA.

Knowledge of TNA is particularly applicable if you are commissioned to provide training for a particular organisation by initially identifying what the people in the organisation actually need to be trained on.

If you are a trainer working with a training agency, it is likely that the agency will carry out a TNA and then ask you to provide a particular training course on a specific area that has been identified as necessary and useful for their client. In this case, you don't need to be involved in TNA but you would still need to know the objective of your training course and what areas need to be addressed. Hence, the knowledge of TNA process is still quite useful as you would know where you fit in the whole process and what is expected.

Training needs analysis is effectively a *skills gap analysis*. The main aim is to find out the current state and formulate a desired state. The difference between the two states will lead you to identify the gap and plan a training programme that addresses it.

A TNA can be initiated based on a variety of triggers:

- New technological change
- Customer surveys and feedback
- New customer behaviour or social trends that require new skills to respond to

- New competitors
- New markets
- A drop in organisational productivity
- New legal challenges

A TNA can be applied on many levels:

- Organisation
- Teams
- Individuals
- Tasks

5.1 How Does Training Needs Analysis Work?

TNA is a *data-centric* approach to discovering skill gaps. The current state and the desired states are parameterised and then quantified for comparison. The result of TNA is a series of actions. In particular, it defines the training activities required to get the organisation from its current state to the desired state. Note that the result of a TNA can also be no actions are required.

A TNA can become complicated if many parameters are considered or if understanding of the current or desired state is cumbersome.

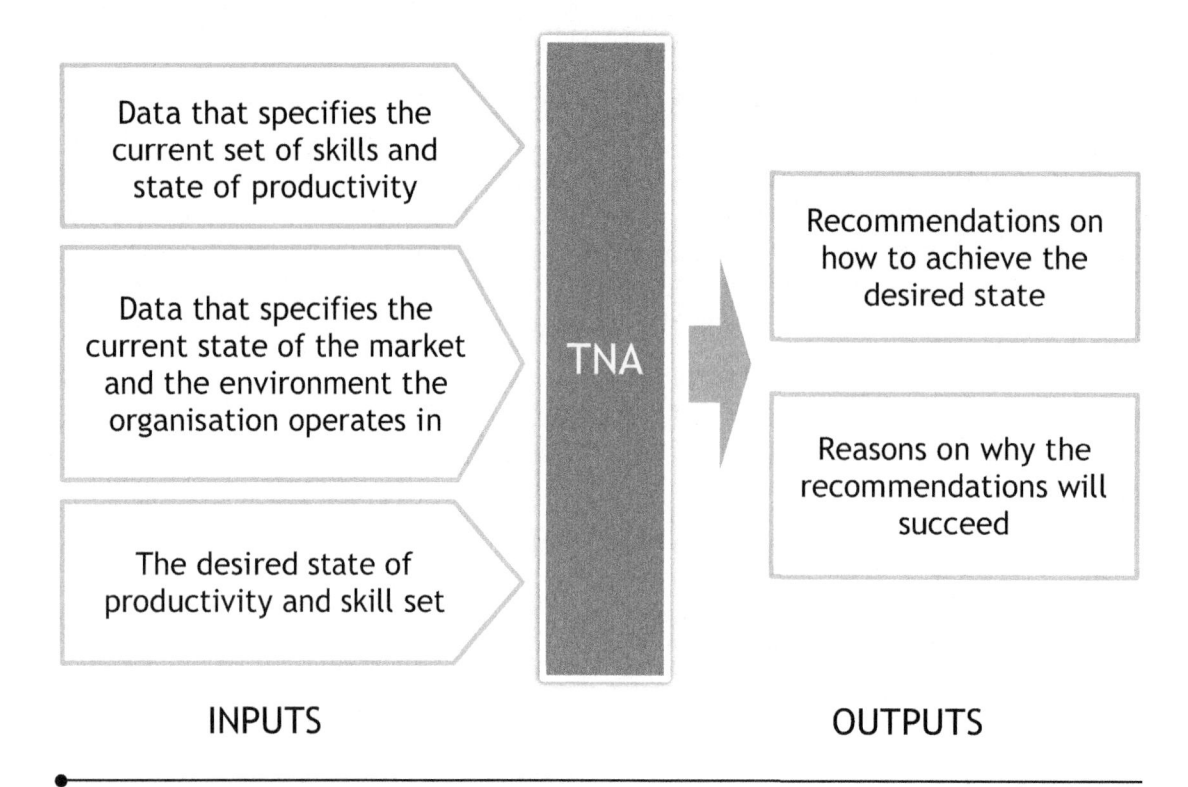

INPUTS
- Data that specifies the current set of skills and state of productivity
- Data that specifies the current state of the market and the environment the organisation operates in
- The desired state of productivity and skill set

TNA

OUTPUTS
- Recommendations on how to achieve the desired state
- Reasons on why the recommendations will succeed

Being a data-centric approach, the analysis highly depends on the quality of the collected data and so it is important to collect accurate and meaningful data. There are various tools at your disposal.

5.2 Training Needs Analysis Data Collection Tools

To collect data for the inputs to TNA you need to consider the three main inputs and ask questions from the stakeholders and the organisation's management team:

Problem Definition:

- What is the problem you are aiming to solve?
- What is the main objective?
- What do you expect to get from a TNA process?
- What is the budget and how does this influence the TNA?
- What are the challenges to carrying out a TNA and the subsequent training needs that will be identified?
- What are the key issues that must be addressed?

Current state of productivity and the market:

To find out about the current state of an organisation, especially in respect to workers' skills and needs, a variety of tools such as the following can be used:

- Direct feedback by employees on their needs and desires
- Decisions based on broad strategy
- Results of a change management programme
- Psychometric tests
- Focus groups
- Questionnaires
- Performance appraisals
- Exit interviews
- Results of a SWOT Analysis

Desired state:

- What is the desired state of productivity? The more accurately this is defined, the more likely that you will achieve it.

5.3 What Are the Stages of a Training Needs Analysis?

A TNA has the following fundamental stages. Often, a few of these stages are conducted simultaneously rather than in series as each stage can feed into other stages and improve the overall quality of the solution by going back and forth between them.

1. *Define objectives.* Define business objectives that are specifically related to workplace productivity and workforce skills.
2. *Define desired state.* Define what the training activities aim to achieve.
3. *Collect data.* Audit the current state of the organisation in respect to productivity and the position in the market (see data collection tools above).
4. *Perform gap analysis.* Carry out an analysis to identify skill gaps. Find training skills that can address these skill gaps.
5. *Seek agreement on actions.* Involve stakeholders in the process to agree to actions identified as part of the gap analysis.
6. *Create a Training Plan.* Produce a detailed training plan that captures who receives what kind of training, along with who provides the training, the training methodology used and where and when these training interventions will take place. See more details on Training Plans below.
7. *Create an Assessment Plan.* Identify how the training will be assessed to make sure that the gaps identified in the skill gap analysis will be covered.
8. *Design Training Courses or Activities.* Once you know the requirements of the Training Plan and the Assessment Plan, you can move on to prepare the training course. You have three choices. You can either buy off-the-shelf ready-made training materials such as those provided by us, design your own from scratch or use previous materials you already have. Ready-made content accelerates the process and also allows you to use the focused expertise of specialists in a specific domain. With your own design you will have total control in matching the training needs of your client, though this often involves more effort, time and money.

It is important to note that you must involve the stakeholders in all stages of the TNA process. Research shows that their involvement and agreements to the plans identified can significantly increase the likelihood of success. In contrast, a training plan that is *imposed* on an organisation by an outsider may not be taken seriously and in fact might even be resisted by management or staff if is not seen to be in line with company's principles or expectations.

5.4 Training Plan

The results of a TNA can be captured in a *Training Plan*. This is a document that describes the required training with details on specific skills and knowledge required for staff. It also includes why such training is necessary to define the objective for the training team.

The Training Plan typically includes the following sections:

Objectives

- *The overall objective and purpose of the training*. What is the training team trying to achieve?

Training Method

- *Training prerequisites*. Details on what is required before training can take place.
- *Training requirements*. Details on what skills need to be trained on. Includes the approach and resources that will be used in the process. This will lead to training curriculum and the syllabus for each training course.
- *Training providers*. Details of the trainers, their expertise, approach, roles and responsibilities. In addition, it includes whether external consultants or specialists will be used in the process as well as any necessary training resources and equipment.
- *Training plan matrix*. Details on the type of training that each employee receives based on the skill gap analysis carried out in the TNA. An example of a Training Plan Matrix is provided in *Appendix A* along with empty forms.
- *Training schedule*. When should each training activity be provided? Training activities can include training courses, e-learning resources, training software, books, websites, training resources, on-the-job training, etc. The schedule includes how long each training activity will take and when applicable where it would take place.

Evaluation

- ***Performance Criteria.*** Definition of key parameters that will be used to judge the effectiveness of the training applied.
- ***Evaluation methodology.*** Details of how each employee will be evaluated based on the identified performance criteria.

Action Plan

A Training Plan is usually accompanied by an *Action Plan* that identifies the tasks and activities and how they are assigned to specific people. A form such as the following can capture this data. An example of an Action Plan along with an empty form is provided in *Appendix B*.

	Target Individuals	Training Activity	Delivery by Who	Delivery When	Delivery Where	Date Completed
Customer Service Skills	Paul, Joseph	Training Course	Sahar	September 10th	In-House	September 10th
Leadership Skills	William	Mentoring	Alex	Over the next 3 months	Office	
MS Power Point	Anna, Erika, Mia	On0Line Training	David	November 15th	Training Agency	
Delegation Skills	Farida, Andrea	Training Course	Chloe	September 8th	Training Agency	September 8th
Handling Difficult People	Louis, Andrea, Jan, Ahmad, William	Training Course	Ben, Chloe	October 10th and October 23rd	In-House	
3D Printing Machine	Anna, Joseph	On-the-job training	Paul	During November	Workshop	

The Training Plan must be accompanied with an assessment plan. This should clearly define the criteria used to assess the trainees and methods used to carry out these assessments. The assessment plan can be included within the Training Plan document or it can be issued as a separate document depending on the complexity of the training. For example, if employees need to be certified on a particular qualification which has health and safety risks, then critical parameters must be identified and assessment must be audited to make sure that people who go through the process have met the objectives of the training.

5.5 Aim to Learn from Feedback to Enhance Your Training

As a training provider you should continuously monitor your training quality to ensure your training meets the objectives.

One way to find out if training has been useful is to see what delegates complain about. The following are the most common complaints:

- *Too difficult*. Delegates complain that some objectives or methods in the course were difficult.
- *Irrelevant*. Delegates complain that some objectives are no longer important, are not related to their needs or are outdated.
- *Confusing*. Delegates complain that some parts of the course don't make any sense, don't fit with the rest or are inconsistent.
- *Too thin*. Delegates complain that they wish some parts were covered more extensively. This can be more content, more exercises or more discussions.
- *Too much*. Delegates complain that some areas were covered much more than necessary and the time could have been spent on something more important.
- *Wrong pace*. Delegates complain that the pace was too quick and they struggled to keep up with the content. They may complain that the pace was too slow and therefore boring.
- *Poor training methodology*. Delegates complain that they were not happy with certain aspects of the instructional method used. For example, they complain that they don't like to be asked to do something without being shown first how to do it. They may complain that everything was described to them rather than physically demonstrated.
- *Poor assessment*. Delegates complain that they did not like the way they were assessed. They could be unhappy because the assessment doesn't represent their knowledge, or they don't like the method used

to assess them. For example, many people don't like roleplay-based oral assessments carried out in front of an audience as it puts too much pressure on them. If delegates think that the assessment is not worthy of the pressure they need to go through they will complain about it.
- ***Poor training environment***. Delegates complain about various aspects of the environment. Examples include poor seats, poor lighting, poor seating layout, room temperature, lack of refreshments, unreasonable parking costs, bad food and lack of freely available pens and papers.

Each time you deliver a course, you may receive some of these complaints. You will need to act on them to improve your next training course. Of all of these complaints, the complaint about the training environment is not directly related to training. However, don't underestimate this complaint as it can influence the overall results. The negative feeling caused as a result of such issues, which can happen even before the course starts (such as difficulty in finding a parking spot), can easily put people on edge and anchor them to focus more on shortcomings and problems. This in turn make delegates more critical of the actual training content. This can then have a radiant effect. Negative emotions felt by one person is spread to other delegates and soon you will end up with a group of people who feel defensive. You would then need to work much harder to train this group of delegates.

Homework

Consider your three most recent training courses. Use the following form for each training course to evaluate your performance. Given the overall reviews you have received, score yourself from 1 to 5 for the following criteria.

Training Course:

Delivered on:

Criteria	Score 1 (bad) to 5 (excellent)	Your Action to Improve Your Course on This Criterion
Too difficult		
Irrelevant		
Confusing		
Too superficial		
Too much information		
Wrong pace		
Poor training methodology		
Poor assessment		
Poor training environment		

6 What Are the Critical Principles of an Effective Training?

Extensive knowledge of a subject doesn't always mean that the person can teach it just as well. Recall the teachers or lecturers you had in the past. You probably had a lecturer whose great knowledge of the topic preceded him but when you attended his class, you were utterly disappointed by his teaching. The problem wasn't his knowledge, but his teaching method. The skill to train people on a specific topic is different from being knowledgeable in that topic.

To be a successful trainer you need to know your domain well but you also need to be good at training. To be a good trainer, you need to be aware of the fundamental principles that underlie a good training course and teaching methodology.

In this chapter, you will learn about these principles which you should memorise and learn by heart. In addition, a number of learning barriers are also explored in this chapter. By addressing these barriers, you can aim to indirectly improve the overall quality of your training solutions.

You will see that many of the guidelines provided in this book are related to each other and are just different views of the same fundamental principles. You were introduced to some of these principles in Chapter 0 on Accelerated

Learning. Here, you will see these principles from a different perspective which will help you to better remember them in the future.

6.1 Didactic Principles

Over the years, researchers on training methodology have identified a number of guidelines that help improve the efficiency of training. A particularly useful set of these guidelines are known as *Didactic Principles* (Cawood, Muller & Swartz, 1982). These principles should be considered during both the design and the delivery of training content. Note that these principles are related to each other and should not be considered in isolation. They are as follows:

- *Purposefulness*. The aim of the training should be shared with the learners. If learners are aware of the objectives, they can strive to achieve it. It also helps to avoid focusing on unrelated subjects, reduces unwanted discussions and motivates learners to push forward with the training.
- *Methodicalness*. Once an objective is defined and shared, learners would want to know the plan to achieve it. The plan should indicate systematically what happens sequentially throughout the course as well as how an effective training environment is established.
- *Motivation*. You should *sell* the training to learners and make them interested in the subject matter. It is particularly important to include this in the introductory part of the course. You could set realistic goals, show that you are fully grounded in reality and understand the world the learners operate in.
- *Individualisation*. People are different and should be treated individually throughout the course. You must recognise that each person's intellectual and learning capability is different. For example, some need to be *shown* how to do something first before they can do it. Some like to first *hear* an explanation for a particular technique while others like to *watch* it being performed. Some like to explore subjects in more detail, while others might want to get to the bottom of something as quickly as possible. You must recognise these preferences and accommodate learners' needs accordingly.
- *Socialisation*. Humans are strongly social and learning can be much more effective in a comfortable social environment. There must be sufficient group work and interactive exercises to allow learning to take place through social interactions. This is particularly important when teaching soft skills. You must always aim to delicately balance socialisation with individualisation. There must be enough group work

and interactions that learners can learn from each other while at the same time allowing learners to work on their own, at their own pace and with their own learning preferences.
- *Self-activity*. Learners should be encouraged to be active in the learning process, both physically and emotionally. A trainer must use engaging activities and exercises so that learners can use their own initiative and creativity while going through the exercises.
- *Lived experience*. A trainer should aim to engage all senses of learners. Use physical exercises where bodily move is required. Physical and emotional involvement can significantly increase the speed and efficiency of learning.
- *Totality*. Various parts of a training course must mesh together consistently. The techniques and skills explored must be related to each other through an introduction or summary and learners must understand how the knowledge of various parts will converge into a whole.
- *Mastering*. A learner must be given the opportunity to master the skill in a realistic situation and know if any progress is actually taking place. This means that the learner must be evaluated repeatedly during the course and be encouraged by praise and positive feedback. This also suggests that the training does not stop after the course and it is a continuous process. This is why managers and stakeholders must be involved for the entirety of the training process so that a complete training solution can be provided for their staff. Mastering leads to the next didactic principle; *assessment and evaluation*.
- *Assessment and Evaluation*. It is important to assess the outcome of a training course and the overall training solution to see if the objectives have been met. This takes us back to the first principle; *purposefulness*. To make sure the purpose has been satisfied, it is necessary to assess the achievements. This includes not only assessment of learners, but also evaluation of the training methodology and also the trainer's performance. Each delivery leads to a number of actions that can be used to improve the next training course. These should cover the subject matter and any necessary improvements required to stay current with the field. It should also include improvements on training methods and their general effectiveness.

6.2 How to Avoid Barriers to Learning

To conduct effective training courses, it is useful to be aware of barriers to learning. You can take steps to eliminate these barriers. When providing training, be aware of the following barriers:

Learning Barrier 1: Learners Are Not Fully Committed

Learners may not know why they need to learn something and quickly forget what they are taught. If you don't examine learners' current knowledge at the beginning of the course, you can end up teaching them something that they don't care about it. This non-commitment would immediately become a barrier to learning.

Learning Barrier 2: Learners Fall Back to Old Habits

If training is not evaluated after learners have gone through the training, there is a risk that they will fall back to bad old habits.

Learning Barrier 3: Training is Conducted under Artificial Conditions

There is always a tendency to train people in simulated environments. This approach needs to be carefully analysed since certain skills should be evaluated in real-world situations. As an example, consider driving; you can train an individual with theory, whiteboard illustration and even a computer simulation. Even with all of these methods, you will still need to test a person's driving in a real car and in real-world conditions.

However, real-world training may not always be possible or affordable, so your aim should be to train people under conditions that are as close as possible to real-world conditions. For soft skills, consider using scenarios, case studies, roleplays and real-time interactive communication to get the learners practice in real-time.

For communication skills, most people complain that they know what they have to say when they are in a conflict or an emotional conversation *only* if they have enough time. Because they feel they are not fast enough they remain silent or say the wrong thing. To train these people to become better at communication, you need to provide a simulated environment with a similar time pressure. If you can create an emotionally charged background, it would be even better though this can be a lot more difficult to create and is risky to control.

Learning Barrier 4: Learners Cannot Immediately Practice the Acquired Skills

If learners are not exposed to the subject matter after the course, it is likely that they will forget the skill and would not know how to apply it under real-world conditions.

For soft skills, this is not a particularly big problem since most people need to interact with others on a daily basis so they can apply the skills they have learned immediately after the course.

However, this is an incredibly important issue when it comes to technical skills. Consider training someone on a particular piece of software and then not making that software available for a month. The learner is bound to forget about the skills and the value of the training is lost.

Perhaps one of the biggest misconceptions is that managers who send their staff to training think that once a training course is finished the training is completed. Consider what happens when the learner goes back to work after a training course and is advised to carry on with normal day-to-day activities, projects and deadlines. The learner will not have a chance to practice the skills learned during the course. A learner needs time to see how the lessons can be applied to real-work situations. Old habits die hard. It requires persistence and time. This post-training phase should also be considered in the TNA.

If no time is given after the course for reflection on a given training, it will be a waste of training budget, time and effort as there won't be any results. Hence, it is very important to plan post-course activities as part of a continuous training solution.

Learning Barrier 5: Learners Do Not Feel Comfortable in the Learning Environment

To learn, one must make mistakes. This is just part of learning. The learning environment, including you as the training facilitator, must allow learners to make mistakes so they can learn from their experiences. Learners should not be looked down on, ridiculed or laughed at.

Creating this atmosphere is primarily your responsibility. You must also police the environment making sure that certain learners do not influence the environment and make it uncomfortable or unsafe for other learners.

> *"A person who never made a mistake never tried anything new."*
> *Albert Einstein*

> *"An expert is a person who has made all the mistakes that can be made in a very narrow field."*
> *Neils Bohr*

Homework

Imagine you are a trainer who is going to teach Microsoft Power Point. You are probably already familiar with this or alternative software for displaying slides. For the purpose of this exercise, let's assume that you are an expert on this topic and going to be training delegates on this software. Your homework for this chapter is to identify specific learning barriers for this particular course. Consider each of the main learning barriers discussed above and identify what can influence the course negatively. Try to be as comprehensive as you can when listing the issues.

Barrier	What can influence the course negatively?
Learning Barrier 1: Learners Are Not Fully Committed	
Learning Barrier 2: Learners Easily Fall Back to Old Habits	

Learning Barrier 3: Training is Conducted under Artificial Conditions	
Learning Barrier 4: Learners Cannot Immediately Practice the Acquired Skills	
Learning Barrier 5: Learners Do Not Feel Comfortable in the Learning Environment	

7 What Is the Ideal Training Environment?

As a trainer you need to take advantage of every source at your disposal to deliver a memorable performance. This includes setting up an appropriate environment which facilitates the learning for your delegates. As always there are a number of best practice guidelines to follow which directly relate back to the principles of effective training discussed in earlier chapters. In this chapter, you will be introduced to these guidelines on how to improve the training environment.

7.1 What Are the Standard Equipment in a Training Room?

Certain tools are now part of the standard repertoire of a training room and you should aim to have them if possible. Over time, some tools evolve and are replaced by more technologically advanced tools (like when projectors replaced overheads). In general, the common tools at this point are:

- *Whiteboard or blackboard.* A surface to write on is quite useful and is essential. One form of such a surface is whiteboard/blackboard. If the room you are training does not have this, you can use a flipchart.

- **Flipchart and coloured markers.** This is standard equipment and should be present in just about any training room. It has several critical benefits:
    - An unlimited supply of white space to write on. Whiteboard and its variants have a finite space and you will need to wipe off once full. With flipcharts, you can simply hang them on the walls and continue on the next blank sheet.
    - Large blank sheets can be used in group exercises for a variety of purposes such as drawing, making mind maps or activities that require a group to work on a piece of paper simultaneously.
    - Flipcharts can be hidden from view when you move away from a subject. This reduces clutter. However, you can easily go back to a flipchart to recall a previous lesson.
    - Complex flipcharts can be prepared before the course which allows you to save time during the course.
- **Blank walls.** It is ideal to have blank walls to hang flipchart sheets. Well-designed training rooms usually have a special rail going across the wall that makes the process of hanging flipcharts easy. Hanging flipcharts on the wall also allows you to use them as reference and refer to them as necessary. Make sure to check if you can hang flipcharts on walls. The owners of the property might be concerned about potential damage made to walls, so you need to check with them beforehand.
- **Papers.** Always have a batch of blank papers ready. You will need them for exercises or as a minimum for delegates who attend the course totally unprepared and want papers to write on.
- **Pens.** Experience shows that many people who attend a course do not carry a pen! Have some spare pens handy to accommodate for this group of people.
- **Projectors and laptop.** Use of slides for presentation and training is now extremely popular. They work because you can efficiently go through a lot of information at the right pace and content level. Before the course, make sure that you can easily operate the projector if needed and that your laptop or tablet works with it.

- *Interactive boards.* These display boards with touch screen capability are becoming increasingly popular. They are particularly useful for teaching software applications or subjects that require a lot of visual data.
- *Internet access.* If you need internet access to show content during the course (such as streaming videos or websites), test the connection beforehand and *always* have a backup plan in case the internet connection is not available.
- *Computer equipment.* If your training course requires delegates to have access to computers, make sure they are equipped with the right software and are ready to be used by delegates. When the computers are not needed, turn them off or move the group away from the computers to minimise distractions.
- *Trainer script.* Always use a script. It can guide you on timing, on what to say, what to ask and how to conduct various exercises. It also helps you to relax because you know that you can always refer to it when needed. This in turn will increase your confidence and improves your performance.
- *Exercise sheets and other training materials.* Depending on what you are training on, you need various tools and resources. Always plan ahead and keep these in an organised way so you can use them efficiently.

> To see if you are organised or not, follow this rule:
>
> If you cannot find an item within 5 seconds you are not organised enough.

- *Camera.* A camera can have several applications depending on what you teach. You can use a camera to capture the performance of delegates and then show it back to them or provide a video so learners can study their own performance after the course. For example, you can use a camera in a Presentation Skills course for this purpose. You can also use a camera to quickly capture a scene, get a copy of the whiteboard before you wipe it off or capture the results of group work. Depending on your needs, you can then print the image and distribute a copy to all delegates.

7.2 What Not to Do

Activity:

Some trainers prepare a whiteboard by dividing it into several sections and write content on each section for a specific part of the course. Their main aim is to save time.

Problem:

The problem with this approach is that some content will be visible way before you need to show it to delegates, potentially confusing or distracting them. Ideally, you should use flipcharts or slides to show prepared content. This allows you to show exactly what needs to be seen at the right time and nothing more.

Activity:

Hanging reference flipcharts in delegate's direct line of vision.

Problem:

You should carefully control what delegates see throughout a training course. Your aim is to focus their attention on what *you* want them to pay attention to and nothing else. Don't hang flipcharts or visual content behind you otherwise every time learners look in your direction they are distracted by the content behind you. Hang the flipcharts or posters at the back of the training room.

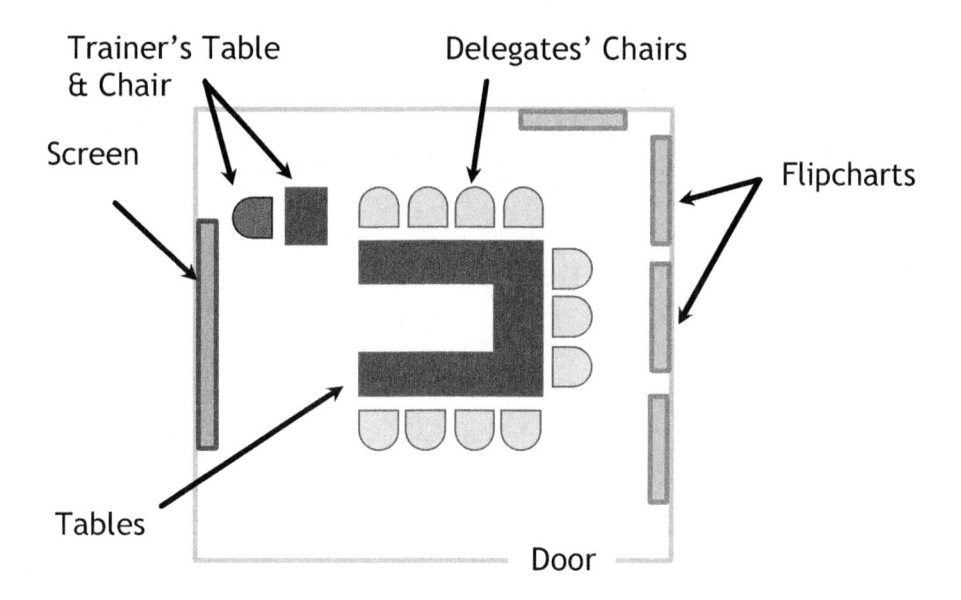

Diagram labels: Trainer's Table & Chair, Delegates' Chairs, Screen, Flipcharts, Tables, Door

Activity:

> Using new equipment, sound recorder, projector, etc. for the first time during the course.

Problem:

> Seemingly standard equipment can actually be quite different, unfamiliar and incompatible. As a simple rule, never assume that you know how something works if you have never used that particular gadget before. Give it at least one try before the course so you are familiar with its peculiarities.

7.3 How Lights Can Make All the Difference

Another critical environmental parameter is lighting. Dim light can put people to sleep. Bright light can be distracting and also gives some people headaches. The most ideal light is sunlight, not too bright and not too gloomy.

For certain courses you can also use light colour as part of training. For example, in a course on stress management, you can use gradual shifts in light colour temperature using specialised lamps to generate a particular feel or atmosphere as you demonstrate key points.

With any chosen method, you should consider how it may distract. Outside light is ideal so long as the view through the windows doesn't distract.

Otherwise, you would need to use an alternative source of light to cover the distracting view.

If you need to dim the light for the projector, aim to dim only those lights near the projector's screen and not all the lights in the room. Do not try to convert the training room into a cinema to get the best visual effects. When training others the main aim is to make sure delegates remain active and engaged in the subject matter rather than starting to daydream or even worse fall sleep. In addition, bear in mind that most people are conditioned to go into a *receiving mode* when lights are dimmed expecting a presentation, a lecture or a movie. Avoid dimming lights whenever you can.

Sometimes you may find that a delegate decides to dim the lights to help out because that's what other trainers or lecturers did. Be prepared to overrule politely and maintain your control over the training environment.

7.4 Keep the Training Room Ventilated to Avoid Sleepiness

Equally important to lighting is a well-ventilated training room. Lack of oxygen and fresh air can lead to tiredness and sleepiness. It is your responsibility to make sure the room remains ventilated. Delegates may assume that their tiredness is due to boredom while it as actually caused by the lack of ventilation and stuffiness of the room. Training room's temperature is another important factor and needs to be monitored and adjusted when necessary. Hot rooms put people to sleep. However, if you need to open the windows, make sure the noise outside is not distracting.

In general, you should involve the delegates in any decision on room temperature, opening windows, lights or level of noise so that a joint decision can be made. This allows you to receive feedback and know if you have provided a comfortable training environment. Don't wait until the end of the course before they tell you that they have been feeling hot all day.

Homework

1. Consider two poor training courses that you have attended as a trainee in the past. Analyse their environment and answer the following questions:

Training Course Number 1

Training Course Attended	
Qualities of The Training Course	
Was the equipment used in the training course adequate?	
Was the trainer organised?	
Did the trainer know how to use the equipment?	
Was the training room well-lit?	
Did the training room have access to fresh air?	

Were there distractive elements in the environment?	
Did the trainer make the best of training resources such as flipcharts, whiteboard, slides, etc.?	

Training Course Number 2	
Training Course Attended	
Qualities of the training course:	
Was the equipment used in the training course adequate?	
Was the trainer organised?	

Did the trainer know how to use the equipment?	
Was the training room well-lit?	
Did the training room well ventilated?	
Were there distractive elements in the environment?	
Did the trainer make the best of training resources such as flipcharts, whiteboard, slides, etc.?	

2. Now imagine yourself as the trainer in the above courses. What would you have done differently?

3. Identify various aspects of the training environment that must change to improve the training course.

8 How to Select an Ideal Training Room Configuration

As you saw in the previous lesson, the training environment can have a significant influence on learning. Another important parameter under your control is the training room configuration. Unfortunately, some trainers don't take advantage of this and go ahead with whatever configuration is available to them which leads to sub-optimal results.

Configuring a room takes little effort but requires planning and foresight. The rewards however are well worth the effort. In this lesson, you will be introduced to a number of configurations along with their advantages and disadvantages and when is best to use each type.

8.1 Classroom

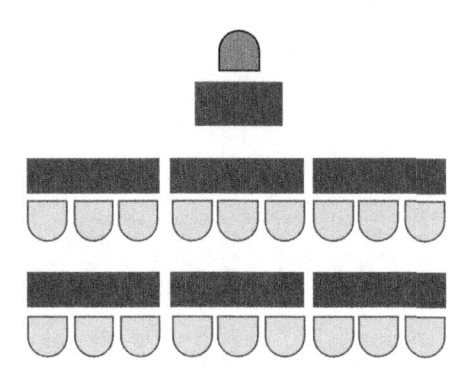

This is a room set with rows of seats. The audience is facing the presenter. This is a particularly poor configuration when it comes to teaching since it discourages interaction between the learners and focuses their attention only on the presenter. Delegates can easily get bored and drift away. Unfortunately, this is still a common configuration in some schools and universities.

This is also a common layout when each student has a computer in front of him and is often set like this for practical reasons. The problem with this approach is that the trainer cannot see the monitors. This prevents him from providing adequate feedback. It is also easy for some delegates to get distracted and the trainer would not be able to spot this. Going behind the delegates is not a good solution as eye contact is lost and is difficult to address everyone from behind.

8.2 Boardroom

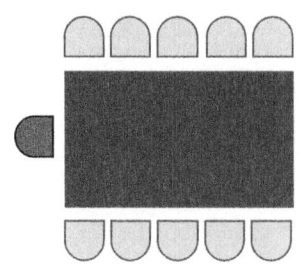

This configuration is the standard setup in most meeting rooms and it is useful for certain activities. It is a formal setup that creates a form of hierarchy much like a board room. However, it is only effective with a small number of people, certainly not more than 7 people on each side. If the numbers are high, people at the end of the table and away from the 'leader's position' will form their own group and some may find it difficult to get involved and participate in conversations.

8.3 U Formation

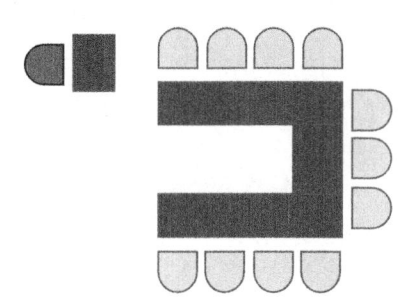

This is perhaps the most ideal configuration for a training session. It has a number of benefits:

- The learners can see each other easily and can comfortably have a group conversation.
- It is easy to divide the learners into groups and let them go through exercises while having a good desk space.
- You can enter the inside of the U and get closer to your audience. This makes the presentation less formal and creates a much better learning environment.
- The room configuration still allows you to present to the class since everyone can look at one side of the room with ease.
- Your table is not acting like a barrier between you and the class as it is put aside in the corner.

8.4 Two Perpendicular Lines

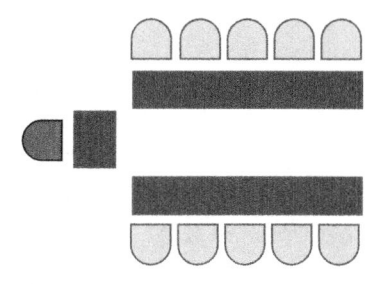

This configuration combines the formality of a boardroom and the accessibility of the U formation. You can observe the work of the learners and interact with them easily. The empty centre can be used for demonstrations or live exercises since everyone can see what is going on. This configuration can also be used for competition between two groups sitting on each side. It is not particularly ideal if delegates need to have a computer screen in front of them.

8.5 Backward Perpendicular Lines

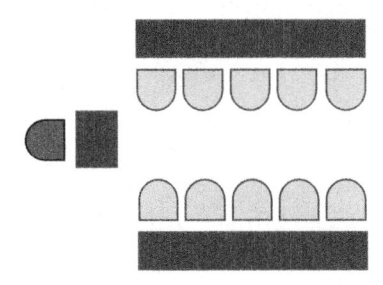

This is similar to the previous configuration except that delegates face the walls. This is ideal when each delegate has a computer screen in front of him. This allows you to see all monitors while providing necessary feedbacks. The layout encourages each row of people to work together and help each other. You can easily address the group by standing in the middle as delegates can turn to face you.

8.6 Circular Formation

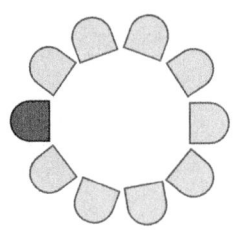

In this configuration everyone is treated equally including you, the trainer. It encourages openness and reduces the formality. This configuration is particularly common in motivation classes or rehabs where the audience is encouraged to be open and to share what they have on their minds. There is no table at the centre which can act as a barrier.

8.7 Circular Table

This is similar to the circular formation expect that the participants now have a table as desk space. This is useful when the learners need to do some exercises or take notes. But at the same time it keeps the interactions informal and open. Your role is usually to facilitate rather than directly present or teach.

8.8 Half Circle

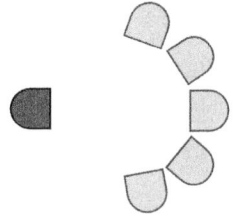

This is also similar to the circular formation and it encourages openness. It puts the participants closer to you but your role is more formal. This is ideal for bonding sessions, team building or sharing potentially emotional past experiences.

8.9 Group Exercises

As a trainer you often need to divide the delegates to a number of groups for the purpose of exercises. An ideal way to create a group atmosphere for each set of people is to separate them physically in different *islands*. You can use circular or rectangular tables and put the chairs around the tables, or you may choose not to use the tables at all.

8.10 Interview Position

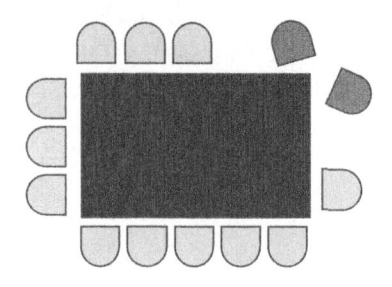

Sometimes you may need to interview a person such as when you want to assess them for performance appraisals. As stated earlier, the usual configuration of a room is to have a large table at the centre with tables around it. How can you use this configuration for an interview session? The most effective method is to create openness so that the person who has been interviewed feels comfortable and willing to share more about his past.

As a result, you want to eliminate any physical barriers between you the interviewer, and the interviewee. Use the corner of the table with slight angles as shown for best results. Do not sit opposite each other since the table would act as a barrier, put a large distance between you and promotes defensive attitude on both sides.

8.11 Informal Chat

This is a common configuration used for informal conversations over a topic with a colleague or a friend. You sit side by side which suggests equality and closeness. If you are in a senior position in relation with the other person, use this configuration to suggest informality and interest in the other person's ideas. The other person will certainly feel more special! This is an ideal configuration when mentoring.

As you can see from the training room configurations listed here, you should not feel limited by the current layout of the room. When attending a client's premises, ask them to configure the training room based on your desired layout. They often need an advanced notice, so plan ahead to avoid disappointment.

Homework

1. Consider the last three training courses you have attended as a *trainee*. Answer the following questions:

Training Course Attended	What layout was used?	Was this layout efficient and appropriate for the type of training delivered?	If not, what would have been more ideal?
1.			
2.			
3.			

2. Consider the three most recent training courses you have *delivered*. Answer the following questions about them:			
Training Course Delivered	*What layout was used?*	*Was this layout efficient and appropriate for the type of training delivered?*	*If not, what would have been more ideal?*
1.			
2.			
3.			

9 How to Start a Course

Imagine that a trainer starts his course by going through his usual introduction. He introduces himself, goes through the emergency exit procedure, explains the agenda and talks briefly about the course. He then swiftly moves on to the first session of the course and continues to lecture the delegates about the topic.

Up to now, the only person who has been talking is the trainer. Delegates are silent. Some might look already bored. Some have crossed their arms and are becoming increasingly defensive. Some of the others are wondering if they have made the right choice to attend this course.

What is going on?

9.1 Handling the Silence Treatment

The trainer seems to have done everything by the book; going through introduction, covering health and safety, telling the delegates about refreshments and agenda and even given a brief summary of what the course is about. So what is missing?

A small training course is different from a lecture. People need to interact with each other and the trainer. They need to share their concerns freely and without feeling intimidated.

> All of this means that you must do something to make delegates feel comfortable. A great way to start this process is it to make them talk.

Talking breaks the ice. People gradually become more confident in engaging others. By making people talk you also make the training much more informal; it becomes a friendly discussion as opposed to a one-way lecture.

9.2 Make People Feel Comfortable at the Start of the Course

If delegates don't know each other, you can use the following simple techniques to make them feel comfortable:

1. Ask Them to Introduce Themselves

At the beginning of the course, ask the delegates to introduce themselves one by one. The most important sound or word in anyone's life is their own name. People love to hear their names being called. When it happens they feel more comfortable with the person who called them.

In contrast if people don't call you by name, they will appear cold and non-caring. It is as if they cannot be bothered to learn more about you.

Given this, facilitate the process so that everyone states their name at the beginning of the course. In addition, use name tags that are easily readable from a distance to help delegates remember each other's names. It can be a tall order to expect everyone to learn the names of 10 other people without any practice (yes, human short term memory isn't that impressive). You can use icebreakers for this purpose. Consider using icebreakers[3] such as "What is my nickname?" or "Name Juggle."

---

[3] You can get these icebreakers and many others for free from our site SkillsConverged.com

2. Get Them to Share Their Background

In addition to names, get the delegates to explain a bit about themselves. This helps to break the ice further by explaining their interests. You can do this by using a Relay questioning technique and ask each person, one at a time, to state their background to the whole group. You will find more on questioning skills later in the book.

If you have a large group of delegates or they are going through a multi-day course or a team building course you may need to accelerate this introduction phase. In these cases, consider using the following icebreakers, all available from our website:

- "Ask Three Questions"
- "Are You an 'A' or a 'B'"
- "Draw Your Introduction"
- "Common Interest"

3. Get Them to Share Their Desires

Next, get each person to explain what they want to get from the course. Not only this allows you to tailor the course, it also encourages delegates to talk beyond introducing themselves, making them feel more comfortable with each other through having shared problems.

> Despite the simplicity and effectiveness of the above techniques, unfortunately many trainers still don't use any systematic approach to make people feel comfortable with each other.

In examining training courses, time and again, we have seen poor results just because no effort was made to make delegates feel comfortable in the environment and with each other. We have seen that delegates go through a course with a defensive attitude, remain silent and are unresponsive when asked questions by the trainer. The poor performance usually correlates with poor recall rates after the course as delegates have not absorbed the content effectively.

9.3 Use Team Building Techniques as a Warm Up

It is possible that you might be running a course where delegates know each other (for example an in-house training session). In this case, you don't need to go through elaborate icebreakers to help delegates to get to know each other. You, as the trainer, may still need to learn their names and needs but the introduction phase does not have to be as detailed as when no one knows anyone else. However, you still need to make delegates feel comfortable with each other and the training session. You can use a variety of team building exercises based on the specific topic you want to teach. Your aim here is a mental warm-up for delegates. You want to make them feel at ease with each other and the training venue.

Here is a selection of team building exercises that you can consider:

- Team Building Exercise: Shrinking Platform
- Team Building Activities for Kids: My Dream T-Shirt
- Team Building Exercise: Helium Stick
- Change Management: Concentrate on Change to Survive
- Team Building Exercise: Make it Square
- Cooperative Teamwork Exercise: Sort the Cards

9.4 Start a Course Like a Movie

Recall the last movie you watched that you really liked. How did it start? Did it grasp you within the first 5 minutes? Were you so impressed that you almost forgot that you were watching a movie and instead *felt* you were really there with the characters?

Some movie openings are truly epic. In movies such as the James Bond series, the first scene before the main title can easily turn out to be the most expensive part of the movie. They start with a "big bang."

So why does Hollywood spend so much effort and money on starting with a big bang?

The answer is that over the years, film makers have discovered that in order to pull the audience in, to capture their interest and to make them switch off from the rest of the world, they must make a big impression right from the start. Before the movie starts (at home, or in the cinema) people are still concerned with their own daily lives and immediate events that are fresh in their minds; collecting the kids from school, sending the important e-mail to a client, buying a Christmas gift for mum, booking a restaurant for anniversary and so on. It takes a while for us to leave our real world behind and become absorbed in the imaginary worlds of movies.

The movie industry, through trial and error, has discovered that in order to pull us into their specific imaginary world they need to do it with a big bang or they may never capture our *wandering* minds.

When it comes to training, you can borrow from the same technique. Aim to impress your delegates right at the beginning of the course to get their attention and help them gain more from the experience of training. This requires an *educational element* as well as an *entertainment element*.

Let's consider this again.

> Starting with a big bang means that a purely educational element is not enough. Unfortunately, this is how most trainers start their courses. Sometimes, they even start with the most boring content.

To illustrate, here is an example of a course on business networking. The trainer begins like this:

> "Let's start with the origins. The word 'network' is defined in the Oxford dictionary, edition 2005, as Network (noun) 1) An arrangement of intersecting horizontal and vertical lines... 2) A group or system of interconnected people or things... (verb) 1) Connect or operate with a network... 2) (often as noun networking) Interact with others to exchange information and develop professional or social contacts. The 1922 edition of Oxford English Dictionary states that network is actually a combination of 'Net' and 'Work' and this is how it has entered the language. It referred to the act or process of fabricating a net from threads or wires. So network is about us working or creating together through our contacts..."

Boring, boring, boring...

You can be sure that by now most delegates are bored to death not to mention that they haven't really learned anything with any practical value about business networking.

This is a poor way to start a course. Instead, you need to understand *why* people attend such a course and then design and deliver a course that

Train the Trainer: The Art of Training Delivery

captivates them and shows them straight away that you are here to teach them a new and useful skill that can help them succeed.

For this example, people might attend a course on business networking because they are naturally shy when it comes to making contact with others, so they want to enhance their interpersonal and communication skills. In particular, they want to improve their interactions with strangers. They want to learn how to make a good first impression. They might be coming to this course to learn where they should go to network with others. They want to know, step by step, how to approach a networking event, introduce themselves and market their skills.

To capture your delegates' imagination at the start of the course, you can explore interesting examples of such events. Describe an event that went well. Describe an event that didn't go well. What is the latest trend in the industry? What are the novel mechanisms that people use to network these days in contrast with the methods used in the past?

9.5 Do Not Apologise for Being Boring

Some trainers think that if they have boring content they should apologise for it. So they start the course like this:

> "I know what I am going to explain to you now is really boring, but you really have to go through this…"

Let's pause and analyse this. What is the trainer trying to do here? Is he trying to justify the boring content? If you have boring content, you should get rid of it or make it exciting; you cannot justify it. Is he trying to cover his back so that he is not accused of teaching boring content? Unfortunately, a warning will not save the trainer, since a bored audience will not learn and will let others know about their poor experience.

But that's not all. Even if the content is interesting to some, this statement is guaranteed to make people feel disappointed and will make them lose interest almost immediately.

If you have boring content, don't apologise for it; instead, think of ways to make the boring content into something exciting and memorable.

Homework

1. Pick a training course from your course portfolio that you provide regularly.

Name of the course:

Examine the beginning of the course. Does it start with a "big bang"? Would it impress the audience so much that they would instantly forget about their daily errands and issues at work and instead pay attention to you and what you are saying?

2. How can you improve the beginning of this course to impress your delegates? Consider the following ideas and answer each:

What would you remove? What would you add?

How can you make the start of the course emotionally more engaging?

How can you make the start of the course more memorable?
Can you talk about something that has an element of shock?
Can you perform an experiment or show the results of an experiment that would impress the delegates?
Can you show a related video at the start of the course that would itself act as the "big bang" including entertainment, emotional and potentially shocking or surprising content?
Can you use props to demonstrate a key concept right at the beginning of the course that would make your audience interested in what you are about to say next?

10 How to Increase the Impact of Training Exercises

As you have seen so far, to make a training course effective you should use interactive exercises. You can engage the delegates in activities that provides them with hands-on experiences related to the skill or techniques under consideration.

In this chapter, you will learn about best practice guidelines on running an interactive course. These guidelines allow you to get a lot more out of these exercises.

10.1 Your Proficiency When Running an Exercise

Know the Exercise by Heart

Suppose you divide your delegates into a number of groups and get them ready to go through an exercise using some cards. Next, you explain to the delegates what they need to do with the given cards, but you cannot recall the sequence of steps in this exercise. You tell them to arrange the cards but then you realise that you should have told them to write something on the cards first before arranging them. Having realised the problem, you tell them to give the cards back to you so you can start from the beginning.

You can be sure that by now everyone will be confused on what is going to happen in this exercise.

This lack of preparation will distract and confuse the delegates and will give a poor impression of your training delivery. Go through the exercise instructions before the course and memorise them.

Visualise an Exercise Before You Run it for the First Time

If you are running an exercise for the first time, try to visualise all aspects of it before the course as part of your preparation. Consider the following parameters:

- Where would the delegates sit?
- What would they be pointing towards?
- Can groups overhear each other? Would this matter?
- Can groups see each other's progress in a particular activity?
- Would this awareness interfere with their learning?
- How should you get them to go through various stages of the exercise?

Prepare Necessary Resources

You need to have everything ready when you go through an exercise. You cannot suddenly pause and disrupt the flow of training while delegates watch you search for the missing form in the pile of stuff you have in front of you.

Before the course, arrange the resources necessary for each exercise in a separate pile. Arrange these piles in a sequence based on the order you will go through them in the course. Once you finish an exercise, remove the pile and put it aside to clear up the area. This will make it easier to go through the rest of the exercises without any confusion.

10.2 Managing Delegates During Exercises

Make Your Delegates Feel Excited

Participating in exercises can be entertaining. Most people prefer exercises over boring theory. When it is time to get the delegates go through an exercise, make the best of this opportunity by getting them really excited about it.

For example, do not say, "Ok, now I am going to test you to see if anyone has been paying attention so far. This exercise is going to be long, but it is part of the course and I am afraid you have to go through it."

This will only demoralise your delegates and makes them feel as if they have to endure the upcoming experience. Worse, it can remind them of exams in school which will certainly make them anxious.

Instead, any exercise can be turned into an exciting event. Many adult learners attending a course are already excited to be out of their offices and doing something new and different. Capitalise on this excitement. Tell them, "Now, we are going to go through a very interesting exercise; one that you are likely to remember for quite some time. I still hear from people who attended my course how much they enjoyed this exercise and learned from it…"

You don't even have to be very specific about the exercise or explain why it is interesting. The mystery of not knowing what they are about to go through is part of the excitement. It makes them curious and more attentive which is precisely your objective.

Provide a Brief Overview

This mainly depends on the exercise. In some exercises, delegates do not need to know anything about the exercise before engaging in it. aside from these types of exercises, you would always need to explain briefly what you want your delegates to learn in the exercise. Primarily, your aim is to let them know what topic you are about to cover and how it would benefit them. You need to make sure that the delegates take the exercise seriously and believe that their participation will help them learn the skill.

10.3 Managing Exercise Difficulty

Explain the Rules

One of the most common complaints about poor training exercises is that people don't know what they are expected to do. When you explain the exercise, bear in mind that not everyone will pick up your instructions instantly. Some may need a bit more explanation or a repeat explanation to help them go through the exercise.

If there are important rules to follow, make sure that people know about them and know why they need to follow them.

Provide Structure

Let's consider an example. Suppose you want to teach delegates how to use a particular computer application that allows them to paint. You want to make them familiar with various tools. To get started, you ask the delegates to sit behind their computers and use the painting application to draw a rabbit.

What do you think happens next?

Some people would be confused, not knowing where to start and what to do. Others, who are more experimental, may give various tools a try. This will immediately lead to a divided group, each subgroup of delegates going off on a separate tangent. Some people engage in experimenting with various tools to make a rabbit and some just stare at their monitors not liking the idea that they are not led by hand. In this situation, you are now forced to spend more time with the second group to get them started. Meanwhile, people in the first group will be off chatting with each other, drawing other objects using tools you haven't covered yet and getting bored.

> This approach only leads to chaos. People who like to be told about the process will feel lost or *overwhelmed* when not led. On the other hand, people who like to explore things themselves can feel underwhelmed. They must be challenged at the right level.

When covering a new skill, use a *structured* approach during training exercises. This allows you to progress the group formally while tracking what has been covered and what has not. You can also get the delegates who know more to help those who need help. This allows to offload some work on your side. This also helps you to spend more time and spot patterns in learning or misunderstanding by observing the whole group rather than spending a considerable amount of time addressing the problems of a single learner.

Let Them Struggle

Don't be afraid to let delegates experience a bit of difficultly while going through a task. The struggle will help them look for new ways to achieve the objective and in doing so they will learn the merits of using the new skill. Just make sure that the difficulty is tailored to the level of the delegates.

Observation of training courses shows that most trainers do not push the delegates far enough, underestimating the learning capability of adults. People in general, are fairly quick at learning *so long* as they know what they are about to learn is worth the effort. As people become older and more experienced, this need to know why they should learn something becomes even more important. If you satisfy this need, you can easily increase the difficulty level of exercises and they will raise their level of thinking and focus.

Avoid Distractions

Only give delegates materials when they need them. For example, if the exercise has three stages and each stage requires two forms, do not give all the forms in one go. This can distract or overwhelm the delegates. Instead, go through the exercise one stage at a time, carefully controlling the amount of information given to delegates for each stage.

10.4 Handling Groups When Running Exercises

Mix and Match Groups

Don't use the same groups throughout the whole course. Mix and match people so everyone gets to work with everyone else. Sometime people don't get on well with each other. By mixing people, you avoid condemning some to be 'stuck' together for the duration of the course.

Use variations of all kinds. Sometimes use groups that consist of either all men or all women, sometimes mixed.

If you have a large group of delegates, you can make this process very systematic and efficient using a tool known as Clock Buddies. You can use our free online *Clock Buddies Tool*[4] to generate a number of disks for your delegates. They can use these disks to see who they need to partner with based on your chosen configuration as they go through a number of

---

[4] www.SkillsConverged.com/TrainingTutorials/ClockBuddies.aspx

exercises. The system allows you to change groups periodically by simply shouting out a number and hence run the exercise very efficiently.

Expect Conflicts

There is bound to be some conflict of opinion between people, especially during discussions. Conflicts are in general a good thing as they show the contrasting views on a particular subject. It allows you to take the teaching to a higher level by involving others and use this as an opportunity to teach.

Beware of Intimidation

Looking over people's shoulder when engaged in an activity usually intimidates them and can disrupt the exercise or the learning process. If you want to observe, do it discreetly and from a distance to minimise this effect.

Running exercises smoothly is an important part of any interactive training course and it pays to study this area further to improve your training delivery.

Homework

For this chapter's homework, consider a training course that you will be running in the near future.

Compile a list of five actions that can improve your performance when running exercises and list them below. Be as specific as possible and provide a strategy and examples for the specific course you are planning to deliver.

Your Actions

11 How to Manage Energy and Pace

From experience we know that if not motivated sufficiently, we will not participate in an activity wholeheartedly. This is particularly important for training courses where lack of motivation can be a show stopper. When people are not motivated, they don't learn.

As the trainer, it is your responsibility to keep the course engaging, making sure that delegates have enough energy to participate and to pace the course correctly.

In this chapter, you will learn about the importance of these factors and the strategies that can be used to maintain a desired level of interest on the subjects you teach.

11.1 An Uninterested Trainer Is Utterly Boring

Imagine a trainer who talks with in a low, monotone voice. He sits at the corner of the room while explaining a subject, looking somewhat tired. When he is asked a question, he is very brief with his answer and moves on quickly, as if irritated that his flow has been interrupted. Overall, delegates get an impression that the trainer is uninterested in what he does. For him, it is just another day at work.

How do you think delegates respond to this kind of performance? It is very likely that they become uninterested too. Delegates can sense that the trainer is not fully committed. As a result, they feel bored and endure the course rather than enjoy it. This lack of enthusiasm can quickly spread and soon the whole class will be unmotivated.

11.2 Positive Attitudes Are Contagious

As a trainer, you must always see yourself as a role model for the subject domain. This is because you are intensely observed by delegates. Your extreme interest in a subject or your natural energy when discussing something that you enjoy will come across and will motivate your delegates to become just as interested.

Remember, strong emotions are contagious. So if you appear enthusiastic, soon everyone else will be too. If you appear bored, soon the delegates will feel the same.

When providing a training course consider using the following techniques to influence your delegates:

- *Use a firm voice*. Use a firm voice that inspires confidence in your skills and your training. Your confidence in a subject will make people trust your knowledge and remain interested in learning from you.
- *Use gestures*. Use enthusiastic gestures and body language to inspire interest.
- *Be energetic and lively*. Move around to project your energy but move in moderation as not to distract.
- *Appear relaxed*. Show that you are relaxed. A nervous and anxious trainer will make delegates uneasy and will distract them. To be relaxed, know your domain well and plan ahead by visualising the training course. The more preparation you go through the easier it is to deliver a course especially if you are doing it for the first time.
- *Appear happy*. Show that you are happy to be training delegates on this topic. Great trainers are at ease and happy with their job, usually emitting a kind of energy that shows their love and passion for the topic. It is as if they rather be there teaching than be anywhere else.
- *Use humour*. People want to be entertained. Using humour shows that you are comfortable with the domain and know how to make training fun and engaging.

11.3 How to Spot Unmotivated Delegates

People learn faster and much more thoroughly when they want to learn. Your aim as a trainer is to create an environment that facilitates this.

Look for signs that indicate your audience is drifting away or is resisting your content. You can then tactfully change your approach to respond to this need. Look for the following signals:

Losing Eye Contact

Sign:

> If you start to see that most of your audience have broken eye contact with you, it is likely that they are losing interest or are getting bored.

What to Do:

- Move on to a different topic which is preferably interactive. This forces delegates to make eye contact with you as you explain how they should participate.
- You can show delegates a demo or a video to encourage them to do something new.
- Imply that what you are about to show will be different from what they have already gone through.

Delegates Cross Their Arms

Sign:

> Crossing arms is usually a sign of defensive attitude. If you see delegates crossing their arms it might be that they are not agreeing with what you are saying. It could also be a sign that they are cold and uncomfortable.

What to Do:

> The mind follows the body in the same way that the body following the mind. By changing their posture, you can also hope to shift delegates' attitude. This means you need to get the delegates to move away from their current positions so they are forced to uncross their arms.

> In an interactive training course, one way to do this is to engage the delegates in an exercise. For example, gather around a separate table and provide props, cut outs or tools which they need to use as part of the exercise to practice on one of the skills taught in the course. As soon as delegates try to participate in this exercise, they will be forced to uncross their arms and are more likely to feel less defensive and more receptive.

Train the Trainer: The Art of Training Delivery

Sudden Introduction of Distractions

Sign:

You spot distractions in the environment caused by the outside world or even by certain delegates. Distractions can lead to a de-motivated audience. For example, if your training class has windows and delegates can see that there is an interesting event unfolding outside, they will pay less attention to you and more attention to what is going on out there. Being opportunistic, people may start to feel that they would rather be outside than inside.

What to Do:

There are basically two ways to handle distractions; prevent them from taking place or address them as they develop.

- *Preventative measures.* You should design the training environment in a way that minimises such distractions. For example, if the room next door is occupied by people who can be overheard in your training class, you need to address this *before* it becomes an issue.
- *Addressing distractions.* Once spotted a distraction, don't ignore it.

To address distractions, do one of the followings:

- *Address the issue directly.* For example, if there is a distracting noise, find the source and take steps to silence it.
- *Involving the delegates in the process.* Use delegates' help in minimising the distraction. For example, delegates may collectively decide that pulling down the blinds is the best way to avoid getting distracted by what is going on outside.
- *Distract them from the distraction.* Sometimes avoiding a distraction is not easy. In this case, carry on to another engaging topic and distract the delegates from paying attention to anything else. Once delegates have forgotten about the distraction you can move back to the main topic while keeping them fully engaged. This method can be difficult if the distraction keeps happening.

11.4 How to Motivate an Audience and Avoid Boring Them

Consider the following guidelines to motivate your delegates:

Use Easy-to-Follow Content

To keep delegates motivated, make sure the content is at the right level for them. This means you should be able to adapt during the course based on the delegates' needs.

The syllabus should not be written in stone. Some trainers think that delegates have to *endure* a training course. Sometimes they even say this up front! It usually goes like this, "Sorry about this. This health and safety regulation is going to be really boring but you have to go through it I am afraid." This doesn't do anything for motivation. Even if they were remotely interested, they are feeling bored before you even start.

Make it Non-Threatening and Non-Criticising

Aim to create an environment that people know they can learn in it. If delegates know they will be criticised either by you or other people around them, they will not be interested to fully participate.

Change the Flow

When you realise that you are about to lose the audience you can use a variety of techniques to gain control. Consider techniques such as an "interactive pause" or the "three minutes pause" which will help you change your pace[5].

Use Energisers

It is possible that delegates get tired mentally during the training course. This problem is more common in the second or third day of a multi-day course. Having gone through complex topics delegates may reach a saturation point.

---

[5] Search for these techniques on SkillsConverged.com to learn more.

Equally, delegates can get physically tired. This is particularly important for day long courses where they will be sitting all day through the course.

Consider your delegates' physical needs and arrange activities that can satisfy the simple need for movement. Moving will help with blood flow and increases oxygen intake. It also helps the body to get rid of toxic waste that accumulates in the lymph nodes during the day. This is handled by the lymph system which does not have a pump similar to a heart that circulates blood around a body. Physical movement helps the body to get rid of waste, which in turn prevents sleepiness or tiredness.

To make delegates move and become more active, you can use a class of training exercises known as *energisers*. Depending on your training environment, energisers can be used indoors or outdoors. Outdoor activities have the advantage of providing the delegates with fresh air. It will get people out of the training environment and stimulate all their senses. Indoor activities are shorter and easier to conduct and if you cannot be outdoors, they are still better than nothing. Here are a number of example energisers:

- "Synchronised Movement"
- "Guess Who Is the Leader"
- "Electric Pulse Game"

11.5 What Is an Ideal Pace?

Research shows that the human brain is actually quite poor in handling a lot of data or details in one go. Our brain is evolved to *focus* as opposed to *scan*. Our eyes are positioned in a way that allow us to deeply focus on something and filter out everything else as opposed to the eyes of a cow that is evolved to scan a larger field of view but with much less focus. This ability to intensely focus on something leads to our great capability in thinking deeply, solving problems and concentrating. However, it also leads to a sort of handicap as we can easily miss something while focusing on something else.

This has certain implications when it comes to training people on a topic. When teaching, always aim to focus on key lessons.

> If you dive into too much detail, delegates will soon lose interest, become confused or feel overwhelmed by the sheer amount of data. They will then start to filter out the training content to manage this information overload.

It is your responsibility as a trainer to adjust the pace of content delivery. If the pace is not working for your delegates, review it no matter how uncomfortable this might be for you. If it means you cannot cover the complete syllabus, then you would need to review the syllabus and focus only on those areas that matter most. The rest should either be dropped or delegates need to study them in their own time. Don't compromise the efficiency of learning for the sake of staying in line with your training syllabus or the urge to cram as much information as possible in a given course.

Refer delegates to where they can find more content in order to free up the training time to focus on important topics—material that the human brain can consume over a short time.

Homework

The homework for this chapter is research. Spend at least one hour researching and reading about motivation and what makes people tick.

You have already been introduced to several areas in this lesson, although there is lot more to human motivation. Study the works of experts in this field and then apply it to your training environment.

Here is a list to get you started. Some are about getting *you* motivated, some are about getting *others* motivated. Either way, they will help you understand how motivation works.

The puzzle of motivation - A TED talk by Dan Pink:

www.ted.com/talks/dan_pink_on_motivation

Motivation hacks by Leo Babauta from Zen Habits

zenhabits.net/top-20-motivation-hacks-overview/

Why we do what we do. A TED talk by Tony Robbins

www.ted.com/talks/tony_robbins_asks_why_we_do_what_we_do

Maslow's hierarchy of needs

en.wikipedia.org/wiki/Maslow%27s_hierarchy_of_needs

Our video on inspirational quotes

www.SkillsConverged.com/FreeTrainingMaterials/tabid/258/articleType/ArticleView/articleId/934/Training-Video-Inspirational-Quotes.aspx

Also consider referring to the list of recommended books in *Appendix D* for further research.

12 How to Manage Expectations

You meet a new friend who is into crafts. She makes jewellery using metal, glass, wood, plastic and a variety of other materials. You have had a passing interest in the area but the way your friend talks about the subject makes you feel very excited about this subject. At this point you are interested, but have no *expectations*.

You visit her home one day and you are blown away. It feels like so much fun to be able to create a piece of jewellery that you can wear or even sell to others. You feel hooked. You are so excited that you want to take this up as a hobby. Your friend, who is very good at making jewellery, shows you a few tricks and you make a necklace with a pendant and earrings right there in her studio. You think you did really well. Later on, when you show what you have made to your friends and family, they cannot believe you have made it yourself and with no previous experience. They think you must be a natural at this. You now expect to be good at this art.

You decide to enrol in a jewellery making course in your local art academy. It is a weekly course that lasts ten weeks. It starts well, but after a couple of lessons, you are not so sure. You find welding to be very tedious. It is also rough on your hands and fingers. Gluing things together is even worse. You feel you need to be so much more patient with it. Glasswork is a whole different skill and you feel like you know nothing about anything in comparison with many of other delegates attending the course. Your expectation is now very low and you feel down.

You don't quit though. You turn up for every lesson on time and put effort into it. Some of your classmates have dropped out already and others skip

Train the Trainer: The Art of Training Delivery

lessons. You feel you need to remain dedicated. By week 9 you are well into finalising your course project and slowly things start to look better. You personally don't feel as happy with the project but you have managed to use several materials together in one piece and your work looks complex and expensive—even though it is not completely polished.

At the end of the course, all works are presented and compared. You look at everyone's work and realise that yours is the most sophisticated piece of jewellery. Your trainer praises you often and eventually declares your work as the best. In fact, she says that she has never seen so much dedication and such good results just after 10 sessions. This makes you very happy. Her praise *exceeds* your expectations. You feel more confident and once again you feel energetic and eager to be spending time on this new hobby.

12.1 How to Empower Learners

If we were to put this into a graph, it would look like this:

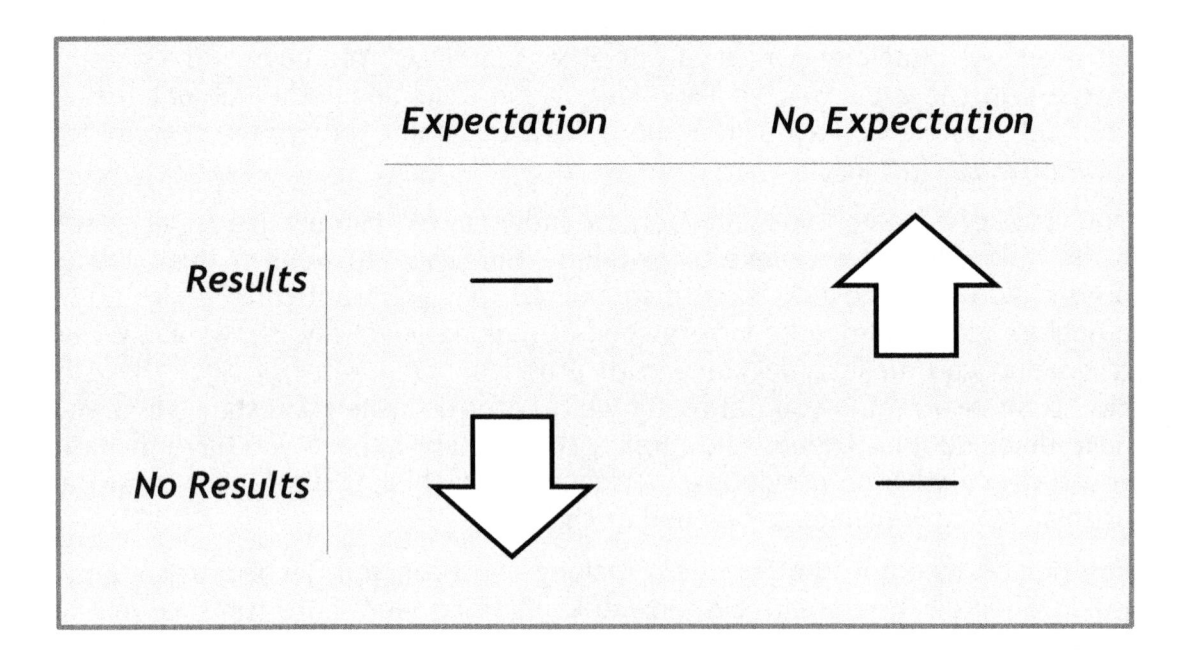

	Expectation	No Expectation
Results	—	⬆
No Results	⬇	—

This graph captures the four possibilities. When you have an expectation and it is met, your energy is neutral. The same applies when you don't have an expectation and nothing happens. When you have an expectation and it is exceeded, you become happier. On the other hand, when you have an expectation and it is not met, you become unhappy. You may think this is rather simple and straightforward; however, the graph leads to an interesting point: You only become happier *when your expectation is exceeded.*

Now let's apply this to the training world. You make people happier by making them exceed their own expectation. Remember, this is not your expectation as a trainer, but their expectation of their own performance. When someone achieves more than they thought they could, their confidence gets a boost; they think positively of the training course, they are more likely to remember the lessons learned in the course and they stay with the topic for longer in the future. Hence, by focusing on expectations, you can control how your training course is perceived.

This may sound rather straight forward. Learners need to have low expectations and they will exceed that expectation one way or another. Unfortunately, this is the wrong way to look at it and can be particularly damaging. In fact, there has been much research in this area with some profound insights.

Psychologists Margaret Marshall and Jonathon Brown asked students to guess their grade in a midterm exam (Marshall & Brown 2006). This is what they observed; those students who expected an A but got a C were naturally surprised. However, in comparison with those who expected a C and got a C, they did not feel any worse. This is because the two groups arrived at different conclusions. The group of students who expected an A but got a C concluded that they would need to put make effort next time to get the A they want. Regarding the group members who expected a C and got a C, it just reinforced their belief about their lower abilities in the subject; they were just not good enough at this, and here was their confirmation. Interestingly, this reaction was similar to another group. Those who expected an A and got an A also reinforced their belief about themselves; they were clever, and this is why they got an A. Some students who expected lower grades but got an A attributed the result to luck.

In principle, people with higher expectations are generally happier no matter what they achieve. Here is a question though. If people need to have high expectations, how can you get them to exceed that expectation so that they feel empowered and happy about what they are doing? Is there an easy way to achieve this?

> To manage an expectation, you can approach it in two ways—help a learner meet and possibly exceed that expectation, or express the expectation in a way that leads to satisfaction.

12.2 How to Exceed Expectations While Learning

Here are a number of strategies you can use to help delegates exceed their own expectations when involved in learning a skill.

Help Learners Define Ideal Goals

You can help a learner set an objective that defines the expectation but in such a way that the learner thinks it is a big deal to achieve it. Meanwhile, from experience, you know that the objective is well within the grasp of the learner; it is just that the learner doesn't know it yet.

With this technique, you encourage the learner to set high goals and hence have high expectations. Simultaneously, you are setting up an environment that helps the learner exceed that expectation.

For example, you want learners to think more creatively about problem solving. You have a particular team building activity in mind that you know most people will find challenging, at least initially. However, as they go through it, they begin to gain confidence and after some sustained effort can achieve the desired results. Examples of such team building activities are "The Helium Stick", "Paper Bridge" and "Don't Break the Egg."

Encourage Constant Awareness of Goals

To achieve a goal, a learner must understand the goal and know how to measure progress. Unlike learners in school, adult learners need to be responsible for measuring their own progress. It is therefore important that the goal is well-defined and the learner's performance is periodically measured to see how far he has come and how far he has to go. This, in turn, requires constant awareness of the objective.

For example, at the beginning of each session set clear objectives. Make sure delegates know what it is they need to achieve. What would be considered a pass? What would be considered excellent work? Why would they need to learn the skill? How would this relate to other skills? While going through the lesson, ask them what it is they are aiming to achieve. Encourage them to verbalise this and bring it to their consciousness. The awareness creates focus and determination.

Prime the Learners

Psychologist Sara Bengtsson carried out some amazing research (Bengtsson *et al.* 2011). Each one of the twenty-one healthy participants in the research was given a series of scrambled sentences one at a time. Each sentence consisted of six words, and participants had to judge whether the words could be arranged into a grammatically correct sentence. There was, however, a twist as participants analysed the set of words one after another. Each set of words was chosen based on a specific condition and directly related to it. The conditions were "clever", "stupid", "happy", "sad" and "neutral." For example, the six words chosen for "clever" were: "the brightest nothing idea everything promoted." The six words chosen for "stupid" were: "welcome not morons one are here."

Therefore, the subjects were primed as "clever", "stupid", etc. and some were left as neutral to act as a control group. Interestingly, the researchers also used an MRI to scan the participants' brain activity while they went through the task.

What the researchers found was quite fascinating. The results showed that those who were primed as "clever" were more successful than those who were primed as "stupid." Those who were primed as "clever" spent more time checking for errors while analysing a given sentence, while those who were primed as "stupid" spent less time. In other words, being primed as "clever" evokes a number of self-concept associations, such as competent, bright and skilled. Once self-concept was affected, people reacted differently to their own behaviour. Those who were primed as "stupid" triggered associations, such as inefficient and forgetful, which, in turn, reduced their performance on the task.

This, as well as other research in this area, has led to profound insight. People who are made to think that they are doing well are more likely to learn from their mistakes and subsequently do better. Those who are convinced that they are likely to fail are less interested in learning from their mistakes and are, hence, more likely to fail. People's beliefs in their own abilities lead to self-fulfilling prophecies that confirm their original beliefs.

> Higher expectations suggest that a learner has what it takes to achieve the expectation. This, in turn, creates a positive self-fulfilling prophecy that makes the learner more capable until he achieves the higher expectations.

Help Them Aim for High Expectations—But Not Foolishly

As you saw earlier, learners are better off if they aim higher; but how high is high? Numerous studies show that forcing people to commit to ambitious goals that seem to be out of reach can lead to massive increase in productivity and innovation. Such goals are known as "stretch goals." A stretch goal captures an aim that is so ambitious people may not be even be able to describe it. In other words, if you know how to get there, you are not using a stretch goal. Do they work? They certainly do according to various studies in this area. Here are a number of examples of how stretch goals have helped with productivity and innovation:

- A study of Motorola carried out in 1997 revealed that when the company mandated the use of stretch goals, the time it took engineers to develop products fell tenfold (Thompson *et al.* 1997).
- Stretch goals led engineers in 3M to create innovative products such as the Scotch Tape (Coyne 2001).
- The development of the bullet train in Japan was the direct result of using stretch goals. According to a study in 2014, the invention of the bullet trains is considered critical in spurring Japan's incredible growth in the 80s (Bernard *et al.* 2014).

However, when stretch goals are audacious or too big, they can lead to anxiety. The goal is too big and feels impossible to reach so it actually dampens motivation and productivity. People don't know where to begin. They feel lost. They become apathetic as a way to control their intense anxiety and stress.

Going back to the training world, this is precisely the feeling a learner might have when confronted with an unsurmountable learning task. This is when you may say the goal is too high, since rather than motivating to learn, it stops learners from even trying as they feel totally hopeless.

To remedy this, a balanced approach can be taken by combining stretch goals with what is known as SMART goals. SMART stands for Specific, Measurable, Achievable, Realistic and Timely. It captures the idea that, to have a well-defined goal you must formulate it in a way that is SMART. To learn more about SMART goals and how they came about as well as further materials on stretch goals consider reading Charles Duhigg's great book, "Smarter Faster Better" (Duhigg 2016).

SMART goals help to define a goal in a way that feels within reach. A series of SMART goals can then lead a learner to achieve the stretch goal.

When it comes to training people, you will need to help them identify their stretch goals. It gives them the motivation to put the effort in and push themselves forward. However, along the way, they must have a series of SMART goals so they know where to start and how to progress forward. SMART goals help delegates learn various skills, integrate these skills together toward a useful end and produce results that demonstrates they are getting better. With this incremental progress towards an ambitious goal, they can believe in their own strengths and that they are getting closer and closer to realise their stretch goals. In other words, SMART goals are a great way to break down a much larger and ambitious goal in a systematic way so that it gives learners a specific to-do list to focus on. This is another reason why it is so important to make sure learner have set objective and know what they are learning and why. This point cannot be stressed enough, even though it is missed by a great many trainers.

Help Them Avoid Low Expectations

When learner aim low, they may achieve it too quickly without being challenged. This can lead to boredom or apathy; they may not care to participate in subsequent activities or be fully engaged that the content is no big deal.

This is a particularly important point to consider when training. Many might have already been exposed to a certain skill and have some preconception. There is also their ego. Take people in management. Generally, they think highly of themselves. When they find themselves unchallenged while going through a task, they may not think that the task was easy; they may think that they are much more superior and informed than the given task. The risk is disengagement and nonparticipation.

You should therefore match the activities and lessons to the potential capabilities of the delegates.

Reframe Expectations

Don't let the learners lower their expectations; instead, help them to reformulate these expectations. This means to find a different way to express the goal. Let's look at an example.

You are a trainer, teaching a course on graphical illustration. You want delegates to aim high and to be excited about the goal. You tell them about an upcoming national competition where they can submit their work. You then proceed to show examples of the work that was accepted the previous year.

Delegates are initially excited about the idea of competing at the national level but as you show several examples, a feeling of despair sets in. How are they going to produce anything remotely close to the examples shown? The examples are elaborate and sophisticated; they are certainly created by professionals who probably make such work every day. How can the delegates produce anything remotely as good?

As you see their despair, the temptation is to lower their expectation. Rather than submitting to the national competition, perhaps they should submit their works to the local art gallery.

The problem is that this lowering of expectation and goal can have detrimental effects on delegates' motivation. Now that it is show in the local gallery, they don't have to put as much effort into the task since it is much lower profile exhibition. In fact, why even bother to go through all the trouble to show the work in a place where the average age of people who visit is 60! Now, with this line of thinking, you certainly cannot expect much from the delegates.

Instead of lowering the goal, consider reframing it so that rather than getting anxious, delegates remain motivated. For example, a new goal could be that everyone must produce a work suitable for submission to the national competition but there will be two stages. They need to exhibit their work first right here in the training academy. Friends and family will be invited to view their work in a private session. The trainers, the visitors and all delegates will then vote for their favourite work. The top three works will be selected based on the votes and will be submitted to the national competition.

So now you have introduced a secondary goal that is more within the reach. All delegates have to do is to compete with each other and be among the top three. The main goal is still valid and leads to high expectation, but since the focus has changed to the local competition, anxiety is reduced and the goal feels much more within reach. In fact, it is as if you have used SMART goals to reframe the big goal and make it more manageable.

12.3 The Gap of Disappointment

When a learner is going through a learning process, there are situations in which he may feel that no matter how much effort he puts into learning a new skill, he doesn't get good results. This can be frustrating, and he may wrongly conclude that he is not good enough to learn that specific skill.

It is actually quite natural to feel frustrated at some point during the learning process. Let's illustrate how this pattern works using the following graph.

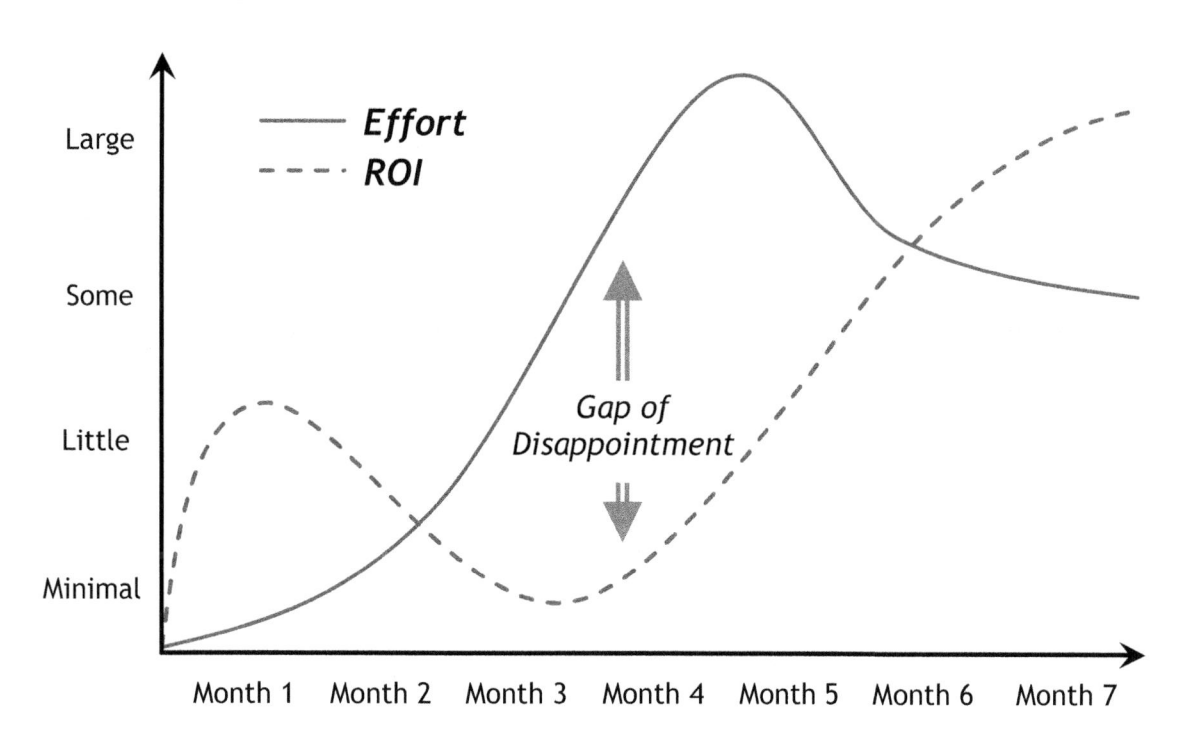

Two curves are shown on this graph over time. One is *effort* and the other is *Return on Investment* (ROI). ROI is a common term used in business, and it often refers to the amount of money that can be made from an investment. ROI can also be used to represent any other resource, such as a person's time. For learning, ROI can represent the results a learner achieves per unit of time spent on learning a new skill.

Let's walk through the graph. A learner starts by putting effort into a new skill, such as learning to use Adobe Photoshop. As the learner is focused on learning this new skill, he immediately starts to get results. Hence, his ROI increases rapidly. He retouches a photo, removes something from the background and fixes the colour balance, contrast and brightness. A few weeks ago, he didn't know anything about this. He is therefore happy. He can feel that he is progressing quickly, and so he puts more effort into learning more.

So far so good.

As he puts in more effort, the learner becomes more skilled. After a couple of months, he is no longer a beginner; perhaps he has reached the intermediate level. At this point, he starts to see the extent of the skill. He now realises that it is actually much more difficult to become a master than he originally thought. He now appreciates what it takes to be good at editing photos in Photoshop, applying various effects and creating extraordinary illusions. He starts to understand what other artists have created with their high-level skills and how difficult it is to produce something similar. In fact, it starts to feel overwhelming. Having got inspired by other examples, he decides to achieve a certain effect, but fails. He tries various methods to get it right, but still struggles. He is putting more effort, but he is not getting immediate results. His ROI starts to drop.

At this point, he may start to feel that the more effort he puts in, the less results he is getting. This is the so-called *gap of disappointment*, and it is in this particular phase that many people feel very frustrated. The disappointment can eventually lead to getting stuck at this skill plateau and never achieving high-level expertise. Some even quit at this point.

Several factors lead to the gap of disappointment:

- **Impatience about learning and wanting immediate results.** This can be because of that initial high ROI, which can make a person think that he will always get the same level of return as he puts more effort in.
- **Delay in getting results.** With some skills, effort doesn't necessarily lead to immediate results. A learner has to be patient until he can see

measurable results. Take bodybuilding or losing weight as an example. Due to the nature of the human body, you may not see observable results, such as a toned body or a smaller stomach, even though your sustained efforts to diet and exercise would have already helped to burn a lot of fat somewhere. You cannot see the results, yet you need to put more effort into it. It means you need to remain patient, focused and persevere.

- **Treating learning a skill as a "tickable" task.** Some people think that once they have learned about a particular area for a given skill, they can completely leave it and move on to something else. Hence, they only focus on learning about new areas within that skill. What they forget is that they still need to spend effort *maintaining* what they have already learned. This leads to disappointment as they think that they are not getting enough return for their increasing efforts.

Continuing with the graph, as the learner stays focused and puts more effort into mastering a given skill, there comes a time eventually when his efforts peak. After this, he starts to see higher and higher ROI until both his efforts and ROI stabilise at a certain level. By this point, he is well established with the new skill. He doesn't have to put tons of effort into it all the time. It comes naturally to him, as it has become routine.

As a trainer, identifying the gap of disappointment of a given learner is crucial in detecting potential frustrations early and addressing them. Often, all you need to do is to make a learner see the returns he is getting. A learner is worried that despite all the effort, nothing works. In reality, he might be getting results, but he just doesn't see it. Your encouragement and feedback about his progress can then help him get over the gap of disappointment. You need to take steps to convince him that his efforts are converting to skills and that although he doesn't see it easily, you can. The boost in confidence can then help him to produce better results, see an increase in his own performance and eventually progress in an upward cycle out of the gap of disappointment.

Homework

Consider the training courses you have delivered in the past and answer the following questions.

Describe a situation where a learner's expectation was low but by the end of the course, he had managed to exceed his own expectations? Did he feel lucky or did he feel that he deserved the results he got? Why did he think this way? Did you do anything to help him feel that the result had more to do with his own efforts than pure luck?

Describe a situation where a learner's expectation was high and the result he got was poor? How did the learner respond? Was he frustrated or did he think that he needed more time to practice the skill?

Should you encourage your delegates to have a higher expectation of themselves or a lower expectation? Why?

How would you encourage your delegates to have a higher expectation of themselves? This depends highly on what you are training them on and their field. Describe your actions below.

You notice that while teaching that some delegates are impatient on getting results. This can lead to the "gap of disappointment"? How can you help them avoid this for the specific course that you run?

Now, for the next series of questions focus on your own aspirations and performance. You are a trainer and want to excel at what you are doing and the field you are teaching in.

What is your own "stretch goal"? What is your next-to-impossible, outlandish goal that gets you most excited?

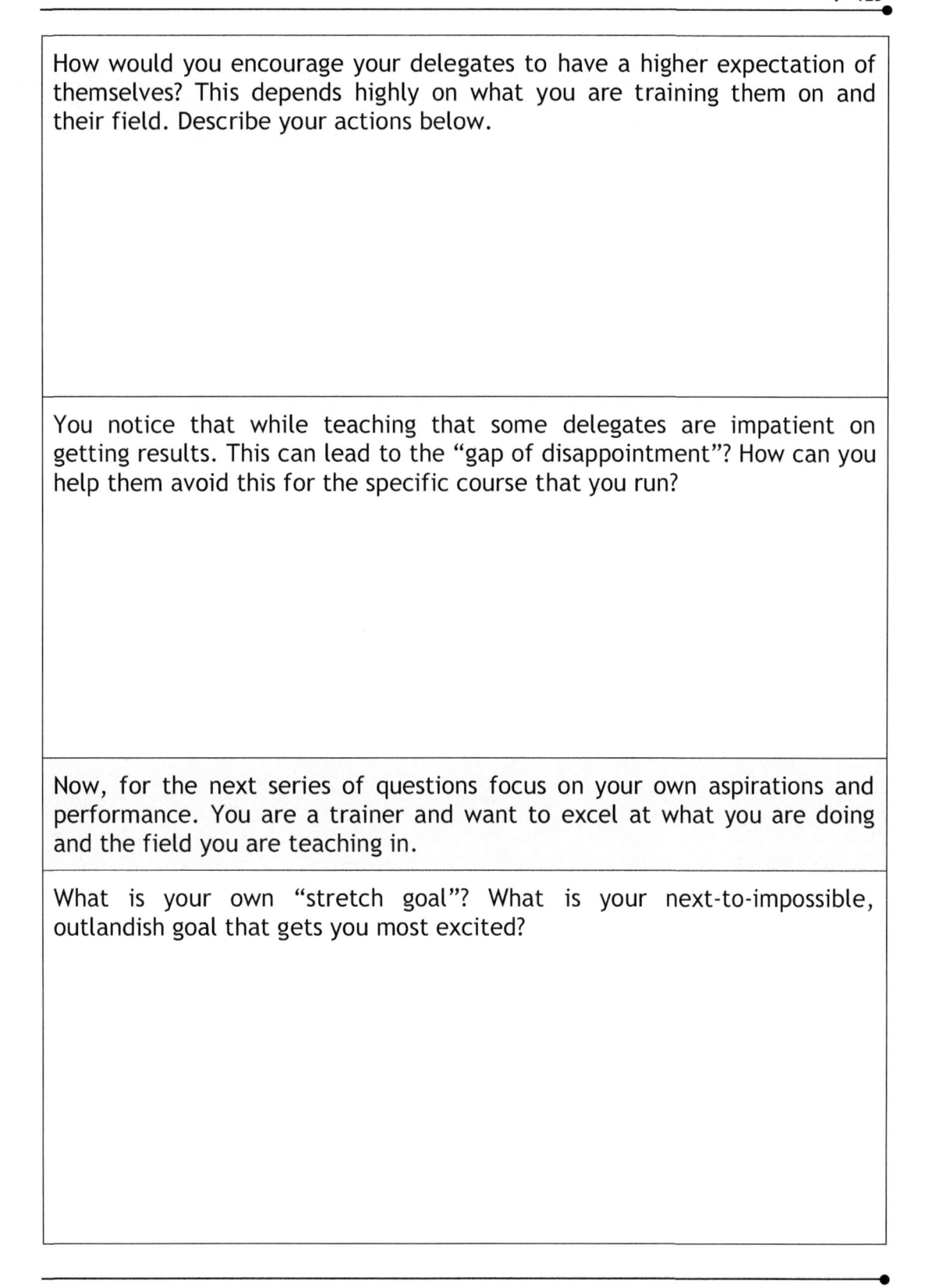

Break down your stretch goal to a series of SMART goals that you can focus on to progress towards your main goal. Use the form below for each SMART goal in the series to identify exactly what it is. Make copies of the form as necessary.

SMART Goal
What is exactly the goal? How would you know you have achieved it?
How would you measure your progress?
What are the actions to achieve the goal?
Is the goal realistic?
What are the deadlines?

13 How to Manage Attention

People's minds can easily wander and if you want focused learning, you need to be able to manage people's attention span. Your task as a facilitating trainer is to focus learners' attention on something very specific and to maintain it. Looked at in this way, you can see once more that a training course is not a one-way communication channel. Instead, you are using everything you can to focus and maintain your delegates' attention on where you want it to be.

In this chapter, you learn how to systematically approach attention management to maximise effective learning.

13.1 Attention Span

Most people have a short attention span and they are bound to become disinterested after a certain amount of time, no matter how excited they are about a given topic. Here is what studies show about attention span:

- *Humans' attention span is about 20 minutes.* Children have 3 to 5 minutes and this increases with age to about 20 minutes for adults (Dukette and Cornish 2009).
- *The 8-second attention span is a myth.* This was largely reported by sensational media. Since this was, apparently, less than the attention span of a goldfish it generated many headlines. This, however, is a classic example of bad science. Let's see what the researchers had claimed. According to Dukette and Cornish, "Continuous attention span may be as short as 8 seconds. After this amount of time, it's

likely an individual's eyes may shift, or a stray thought will briefly enter consciousness. However, these short lapses are only minimally distracting and do not tend to interfere with task performance." In other words, we can get over these short lapses and remain focused.

- ***We can refocus our attention.*** If our attention was fixed for about 20 minutes, we would be unable to sit through the whole two hours of a feature length movie. Since, we can, it means there is something else going on. It is true that our minds will wander after about 20 minutes, but we can refocus. In fact, we can do so after a simple short break. Movie makers are well aware of this phenomenon and they use all sorts of tricks to keep us engaged. An action sequence is usually followed by a calm scene between the key characters. Examples are a romantic encounter or sharing something about past life while sitting by a campfire. Often, not much actually happens during such scenes and they merely act as a filler; they are there to give you time to recover from all the attention you have been giving. Once the break is over, the action starts again usually when something surprising and exciting happens. While sitting at the campfire, suddenly the characters hear the bad guys approaching or the movie cuts to a different location and you are thrown back into the action again.
- The following increase attention span:
    - ***Intrinsic motivation.*** Delegates pay attention and learn a lot more if they are internally motivated than if they are going through a task for an external reward or to avoid punishment (Lepper *et al.* 1973).
    - ***Joy.*** When delegates are enjoying what they are going through they are more likely to pay attention and learn.
    - ***Not too difficult.*** Delegates have a longer attention span when performing a task that is easy or just at the right level of challenge than when engaged in a very difficult or seemingly impossible task.
- The following lowers attention span:
    - Tiredness
    - Hunger
    - Noise distraction
    - Emotional stress
    - Visual distraction

How can you apply such findings to your training? To start, treat a training course much like a movie. Focus on what needs to be covered for 20 minutes and then give delegates a break. Then resume with something exciting right from the start and continue for another 20 minutes.

Here is another example. In a life drawing course, learners draw for 20 minutes and then pause. Learners can now reflect or just chat with others. After about five minutes they return and resume the drawing task.

Now if you are a trainer and you are short of time, the one thing you should not do is to skip a break and go for 40 minutes of sustained effort. This way you will stretch people's concentration and they are more likely to make mistakes and feel frustrated and often learn very little.

If you are short of time, go for a 20 minutes session, a 5 or 3 minutes break and then a 15 minutes session. Don't skip breaks thinking that this way you are maximising learning by getting learners to spend more time on the task.

A session on a given topic may require more than 20 minutes. What should you do then? Let's explore this in more detail.

13.2 Manage Energy, Not Time

One of the biggest concerns of many trainers is timing, staying on schedule and sticking to a plan that was devised before the course.

It is important to start and finish a course at the right time but anything that happens in between should not be set in stone. People are different and learn at different rates. Some people may know a subject well but be totally new to another. Preplanning the amount of time you need to spend on a given session is most often futile.

As usual, many trainers are oblivious to this key point. They bring a training script with themselves that has precise timing notes down to the minute. They know in advance that from 11:30 to 11:40 they will be covering a specific topic mentioned in the notes. This is way too precise. What if you had to spend a few more minutes just before to make sure delegates understood the previous topic? What if you were late due to an earlier discussion that took place at the beginning of the course while you were covering a topic that you felt your particular delegates needed to learn more about? What if your delegates were tired? You cannot force everybody to keep up so that you can stick to your own schedule. The habit comes from following a rigid agenda when presenting a lecture. A training course is not a lecture though. Aim to use rough agenda so you know what general topics need to be covered in which blocks of time. Keep it intentionally imprecise as not to develop a habit of pushing ahead at all costs.

There are however some exceptions: If you have something external such as a demo planned, or have invited an expert for a certain topic, you may need to stick to a specific schedule for that. This should still be kept to a minimum so that you can remain flexible with timing throughout the course.

In fact, a good way to approach this is that rather than focusing on managing time, you should focus on managing delegates' energy. The aim is to increase productivity. You want delegates to learn the most and retain the most per unit of time spent in training. The more energetic and focused delegates are, the more they can get out of the course.

What should you consider in managing the energy? According to Tony Schwartz, people have four different types of energies (Schwartz 2010):

- *Physical energy.* How does your body feel?
- *Mental energy.* How focused are you?
- *Emotional energy.* How happy are you?
- *Spiritual energy.* Why are you doing what you are doing?

As a trainer, you need to keep track of all four areas to make sure delegates remain productive. Here are some examples for each area:

- *Physical energy*
    - Are delegates physically fit to go through the course?
    - Are their signs that show delegates are getting physically tired and need a break?
    - Are delegates sleepy?
    - Are delegates thirsty?
- *Mental energy*
    - Are delegates tired because of engaging in too many problem solving exercises without much rest?
    - Are delegates tired due to previous work deadlines?
    - Are delegates bored because they cannot connect with the topic?
- *Emotional energy*
    - How happy and enthusiastic are delegates while attending the course?
    - Are delegates preoccupied with a stressful situation unfolding at work?
    - Are delegates preoccupied with miscommunication and friction within their teams?
    - Are delegates suffering from office politics?
- *Spiritual energy*
    - Why are they doing what they are doing?
    - Do delegates know why they are learning the current topic?
    - Are delegates committed to the course and the need to go through it?
    - Are delegates positive and participative?

o Do delegates feel they are part of a likeminded community with shared interest?

By monitoring these four areas, and by dynamically allocating time to different areas you have a better chance of managing delegates' overall energy levels. If their emotional or spiritual energy is low, you may need to spend more time explaining why they need to learn certain topics. If their physical energy is low, you may need to skip some content and go for a break. If delegates' mental energy is high, get them to go through more challenging exercises to convert their energy into something useful. In short, you can only have a rough agenda for the course. Don't ever use a trainer script with timing notes down to the minute for every part of the course. You will never be able to follow it and if you somehow manage to do, you are probably doing something else wrong.

13.3 Chunking

Learning is done incrementally. Learners need to take small focused steps. An important technique to consider to manage the energy levels and facilitate learning is known as "chunking."

To use chunking, break down the subject into a series of distinct subtopics. Let delegates know what these topics are at the beginning and periodically throughout the course as you review their progress. For example, say, "You are going to learn X first, then Y and then Z." Sometime later, you can say, "So far you have learned X and Y and now you are going to learn Z."

As you saw earlier, you need to consider humans' attention span of 20 minutes. What should you do if you have sessions that last longer? A good way to approach this is to combine both needs. Spend a maximum of 90 minutes on one or two sessions and then have a break for about 15 minutes. Define the objective at the beginning of the session and at the end check with delegates to make sure the objective has been covered. In between, focus on each subtopic for a maximum of 20 minutes before concentration and focus drop significantly. After each subtopic, have a mini-break.

Here is how it looks like:

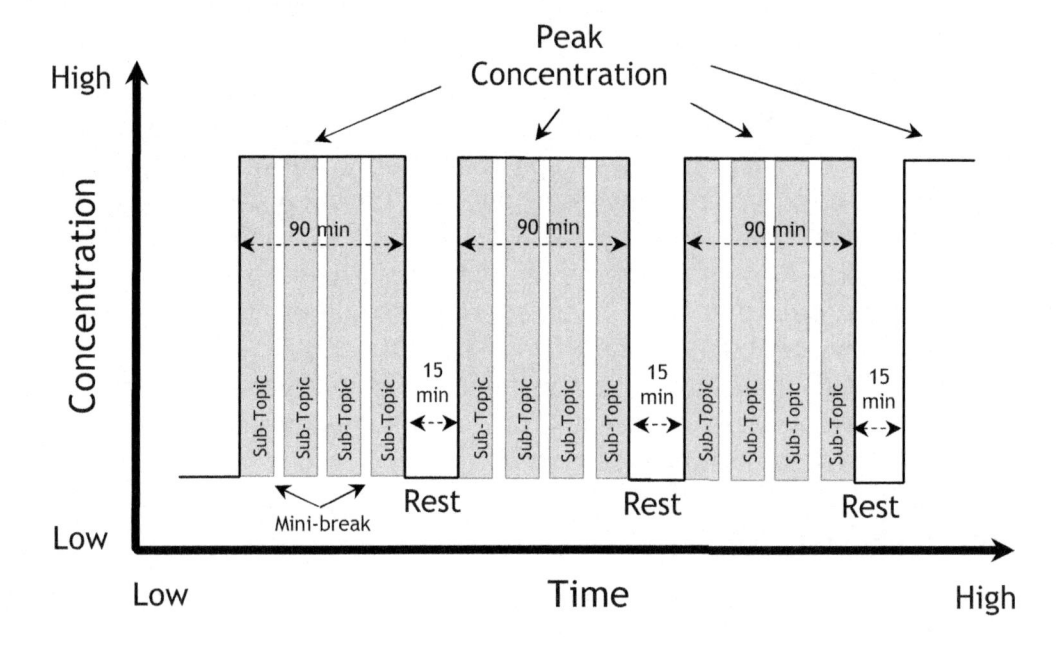

[Figure: Concentration vs Time graph showing three 90 min blocks of Sub-Topics separated by 15 min Rest periods, with Mini-breaks between Sub-Topics and Peak Concentration indicated at the top of each block]

The break can be *direct* where delegates have refreshments and re-energise. It can also be *indirect* using tricks much like the movie industry. Delegates may not be aware that you are leading them through a break, but you facilitate the process so that their brains have time to recover and you can refocus them on the next topic. Let's explore a number of such strategies that you can employ.

13.4 How to Raise Interest and Gain Attention

Strategies to gain attention can be divided to two categories; those that gain attention for longer and those that are short term. If given a choice, you should always aim for long term methods. Use short term when you cannot use any of the long terms strategies or when you need to get through a phase such as finishing the current session before going for a long lunch break. Here are a number of examples for each type:

Long term strategies to gain attention:

- Tell an engaging, powerful and relevant story
- Help learners do something that exceeds their expectations
- Surprise them with novel content such as discoveries, results, techniques and tools

- Show how something can be done easier or faster than they think it can
- Analyse a masterpiece in a given subject
- Get learners involved so they use all their senses
- Give a demonstration
- Ask learners to go through an exercise
- Get learners to do a different activity
- Switch to a different topic and start it enthusiastically

Short term strategies to gain attention:

- ***Gain attention by doing something different.*** For example, move to a new position in the room.
- ***Entertain.*** Tell a joke to lighten up the mood and wake up those people who might be falling sleep. It helps as a quick mental break but be sure to swiftly go back to the main topic as not to get side tracked.
- ***Raise curiosity.*** For example, share an interesting story or use an unusual prop to demonstrate something visually.
- ***Write something on a flipchart to explain a concept and gain learners' attention.*** Do this when you don't normally need to explain the topic by writing it on a flipchart.
- ***Go through a roleplay.*** A roleplay always breaks the pace and helps learners to refocus. It is also entertaining for people to watch. Always use volunteers and make sure they are happy to go through it.

13.5 What to Do During the Breaks?

Ideally, during the break time delegates need to be distanced from the topic and away from the environment. New sensory stimulus helps to make the break feel much longer. So encourage delegates to leave the room if possible and get some fresh air. Provide refreshments and hot drinks. Don't let the delegates continue with the discussions from the training session. They can always do that after the break. It is certainly ok if they want to share their excitement about what they just went through or share their thoughts. But there should not be any deliberate learning or problem solving during a break time.

A main point to consider is that during the break time, delegates should not think about work either. Strongly discourage calling the office or checking emails during the break. This will shift their attention and suddenly they will remember all the stress and anxiety associated with everything taking place at work. The risk is that when they return to the course, their minds will still be engaged with some other area and will become a strong source of distraction and daydreaming rather than being fully immersed in the course.

Unfortunately, this happens way too often. Mobile phones, with all their benefits, are a menace in this case. You simply need to make the delegates aware of this important point. Right at the beginning of the course, explain that you aim to maximise the learning and there is a technique to this. You want them to be immersed in the topic. To get there, ask them to refrain from using their phones for the duration of the course. Just turn them off completely or at least put them in "flight mode." The aim is to have zero notifications and hence no mental distractions or interruptions. It is going to be ok; they can survive a day without their phones.

13.6 Types of Attention

Attention is often the starting point to other cognitive functions. By paying attention to something, you bring it to consciousness and you can then start processing it. There are four types of attention (Dukette and Cornish 2009):

Sustained Attention

This covers the ability to focus on a specific task for a continuous period of time without getting distracted.

For example, consider a course on learning how to touch type. An example of sustained attention is when a learner is concentrating to type as fast as possible with minimal number of typos.

Sustained attention is the highest form of focus. You will need sustained attention every time you need the delegates to go through a challenging task. All other three types of attention are less focused. So if the learning activity requires utmost attention, you will need to avoid the other types. The key point here is that in order to maintain sustained attention, the learner needs to be able to refocus on a task once distracted. As a trainer you will need to eliminate that distraction so that refocusing is not required again.

Selective Attention

This covers the ability to select from among a set of stimuli and focus only on one while filtering out all others.

Selective attention is less focused than sustained attention. Selective attention is a skill. Some people are better at this; for example, they might be working in a noisy environment of an open office and over time learn to block out noise and other distractions so they can focus on the job. This may not be the case for everyone so you will need to be wary of this especially when you get the delegates to go through exercises. Some people cannot tolerate too much noise and quickly get irritated and lose concentration.

Suppose you divide the delegates to several groups while going through exercises. If you have one group who is loud and distracting, others will need to engage in selective attention. Since ideally you want them to have sustained attention, you will need to take steps to minimise such disruption. You can isolate groups so they don't easily overhear each other or you can just ask everyone to speak more quietly but do so in a comfortable way so that being quiet itself doesn't disrupt their attention.

The other way to approach this is to train people to remain focused while in the presence of distracting stimuli. You can devise exercises with small amount of stimuli and then gradually ramp up the distraction in a controlled manner to help delegates adapt and learn. This could take time though and may not be suitable for short courses.

Alternating Attention

This covers the ability to switch focus back and forth on tasks that have different cognitive demands.

Alternating attention is less focused than selective attention. For example, you are training people to use a particular software. While sitting behind computers you decide to show a video of how some features of the software work. The delegates will then need to imitate what's shown in the video in the software on their computers. For this, they alternate attention as they focus on the video and then focus on the software and then back and forth.

Another example is reading a set of instructions on how to implement a particular effect in Photoshop or carrying out a calculation in a spreadsheet and then following the instructions.

With alternating attention, the risk is that focus might be lost every time attention is switched. To avoid the risk, it might be better if you help delegates go through the tasks sequentially if possible so they can have sustained attention in one area and then in another. This might not be much of a problem with related tasks but can become important when the two tasks are completely different, covering two different topics.

Divided Attention

This covers the ability to simultaneously pay attention to two or more tasks with different cognitive demands. This is also known as multi-tasking

This is perhaps when we have the least amount of focused attention since it is divided between several tasks. In reality, the brain cannot process two things at the same time, so divided attention is a form of a very rapid alternating attention.

Numerous research shows that when in this mode, none of the tasks get enough attention, no matter how hard we try. A classic, and a very serious example, is using mobile phones while driving. It has been shown that texting and driving or even having a phone conversation while driving reduces attention paid to the driving task which can have dire consequences.

Certain tasks may require such divided attention as you may need to do several things at once. For example, operating certain machinery, or even driving itself involves a lot of multi-tasking.

In most cases, when it comes to training, you should avoid divided attention and use methods that can lead to sustained attention. The only exception is when the skill under consideration itself requires divided attention. In such cases, you often isolate a number of skills and get the delegates practice each skill separately using simulated exercises so they can have sustained attention while learning each skill. After a certain level of proficiency, you can gradually move them towards multi-tasking and combining all skills together.

Homework

Consider a recent course you attended as a trainee. Evaluate your energy level throughout the course by answering the following questions. For each question:

1. Score the trainer from 1 (Poor) to 5 (Excellent).
2. Describe the actions that you thought contributed strongly to the score you have given.
3. How can you apply what you have learned from this course to your own training courses?

How would you evaluate the performance of the trainer in helping you maintain a positive *physical energy*? Consider physical requirements such as hunger, thirst, need for a toilet break or need for fresh air.

How would you evaluate the performance of the trainer in helping you maintain positive *mental energy*? Consider delegates' engaging problems, deadlines, preoccupation with other areas, mental tiredness and boredom.

Train the Trainer: The Art of Training Delivery

How would you evaluate the performance of the trainer in helping you maintain positive *emotional energy*? Consider actions that helped manage stress, enthusiasm and preoccupation with office politics.

How would you evaluate the performance of the trainer in helping you maintain positive *spiritual energy*? Consider actions that helped define purpose, commitment to the subject, positivity and feeling of belongingness to a likeminded community.

14 How to Manage Learning

How do people learn something? Why some people seem to be good at learning while others are not? What helps to increase learning? These are big questions with complicated answers. Nevertheless, as a trainer, your primary aim is to maximise learning. It is therefore useful to know how learning works and what recent studies show in this area. Knowing learning also helps you to train yourself so there is a dual benefit here.

In this chapter, you will learn about the brain processes involved in learning and will be given a number of guidelines on how to improve the longevity of lessons taught to delegates.

14.1 The Great Brain Transformation

It has long been believed that people who are exceptionally good at a particular skill are good at it purely because they are gifted in one way or another and their skills cannot be topped by mere ordinary men. This belief is so strong that, even today, many people still think it is true.

However, research conducted in the past thirty years has changed our view of mastery forever. This research has been captured in several popular science books promoting new insights and shedding more light on this fascinating topic. Why do some people go on to become elite while others do not (Greene 2012)?

The research on mastery is, of course, highly related to what we now understand about how our brains work. In cognitive science, two contrasting terminologies are used to describe the processes within the brain (Goleman 2013):

- ***Top-down.*** This refers to mental activity which is carried out mainly within the neocortex, which is located at the top and front of the brain. It can monitor or impose on subcortical activity. It deals with voluntary, effortful behaviour. It has control over automatic behaviour, can learn new models of the world and makes new plans. It is responsible for willpower and intentional choice. From an evolutionary standpoint, this is a fairly new addition to the brain; it took place about 100,000 years ago.
- ***Bottom-up.*** The lower part of the neural machinery, which is located right at the top of the spinal cord, deals mainly with routine; involuntary, automatic and emotional behaviour; and as our mental model of the world. It is fast in brain time, operating in milliseconds. This is a much older part of the brain, and it has evolved for our basic survival.

On balance, the brain prefers to go through its cognitive effort using the bottom-up approach, and it does this for a good reason; it costs more energy to use the top-down approach. As you go through a routine several times, some parts of the brain (in particular, the basal ganglia) start to take over the task from other parts. This then helps the brain to spend minimal effort and energy to achieve the same result. As we practise more, the routine requires less and less effort. It becomes more automatic until its takes no effort at all, much like riding a bike or hitting tennis balls with a racquet. Once you have practised it countless times, you may even remain oblivious to the effort that goes into hitting that tennis ball. You will then be able to focus on other aspects of the tennis game you are playing, such as which direction to hit the ball based on your strategy and guessing what your opponent will do as a result.

Learning requires you to practise enough that rather than using your top-down approach, you can utilise the bottom-up approach, which is much faster and takes less effort. To master something, you need to have practised a task so many times that your basal ganglia starts to take over and carry out the task in routine mode. While faster to execute, this will also free up top-down thinking and allow you to carry out additional analysis. This is why there is a fundamental physical difference between the brain of a master who has gone through extensive practice in a specific area and that of an enthusiast who is still learning and must think about every step of the way. This is why it is very difficult to compete with a master without having gone through a similar extensive training experience. Another way to look at this is that once you have reached the mastery level, you become irreplaceable.

This is also why you can't cheat your own brain. Utilising the bottom-up approach and freeing up the top-down approach takes a specific amount of sustained deliberate practice over a long period.

Hence, when it comes to training people, you need to consider a number of key points:

- A learner can become an expert by engaging in "deliberate practice" over an extended period of time. To practice deliberately, a learner must focus on things he does not know—not on areas he knows. You should help learners push beyond their comfort zones and engage in a sustained and concentrated practice.
- You must measure learning. Learners must be aware of their performance. If you cannot measure it, you cannot improve it.
- A learner needs to practice tasks beyond his current level of competence and comfort. There are no shortcuts. No pain, no gain.
- Instinct and intuition come once a learner becomes an expert, not before. Intuition comes as a result of deliberate practice.
- A learner must be mentally engaged with the task to progress forward. If a learner is not aware of what he is doing and why he is doing it, he is unlikely to leave the comfort zone.
- As a trainer, you must coach and mentor the delegates by providing customised feedback about their performance. You should provide the necessary tools and guide learners in a direction that shortens the learning process, otherwise a learner can learn everything on his own given an unlimited amount of time.
- A good trainer is one that identifies areas that need to be improved and advices accordingly to help a learner move to the next level. A bad trainer pushes too hard before the learner is ready, potentially putting the learner off.
- A good trainer is not there just to encourage and say how well a learner is doing; a good trainer is one who helps a learner challenge himself systematically and progress forward one level at a time.
- You must use the immense power of repetition. With repetition the brain can rewire so that it can utilise the much faster bottom-up machinery rather than the top-down.

14.2 Allow Delegates to Make Mistakes

What happens when you make a mistake? You get told off. What happens when you discover someone else has made a mistake? You tell them off. It has been stated that you may hear "No" hundreds of thousands of times while growing up. This negativity and verbal punishment makes us very paranoid about making any mistakes to the point that we get obsessed about making no mistakes at all. Even if we do, we become immediately defensive and will try to deny any wrongdoing.

As you can imagine this attitude can be quite destructive for all areas of life. The reality is that we learn by making mistakes. We don't know a lot. We try to imagine and visualise what happens when we take certain actions. We cannot always be accurate and that is when we make mistakes. It's only by examining the mistake and comparing it to our current world view that we learn something new. With the new understanding and perhaps a new theory we aim to reduce our mistakes in the future.

Mistakes are part of the learning process. You cannot learn without making mistakes. Unfortunately, mistakes are demonised. Rather than wanting to experiment and make mistakes, people want to follow a path that has the most obvious results and the least risk of making mistakes. This hampers learning. As a trainer you should constantly be mindful of this important issue and work around any preconceptions your delegates might have about making mistakes.

Consider the following guidelines:

- *Give delegates a chance to correct themselves*. Set up the environment in such a way to allow delegates to make mistakes. A training course is a controlled environment so there should never be a problem for delegates to make mistakes. For example, use simulation, software, props and custom tools to let the delegates make mistakes safely and systematically in order to learn.
- *Don't put people on the spot*. Let's look at a classic example like a roleplay. If you get two people and ask them to roleplay in front of the whole class, some find the experience quite daunting especially if they have to perform correctly. Performance pressure as well as fear of looking stupid can make people feel agitated. Now contrast this with pairing up delegates and asking each pair to roleplay an activity. Then bring all groups together and ask them share their experiences. This time, people in pairs don't feel they are under scrutiny and can focus on the actual roleplay and the lessons they need to learn. They

are free to make mistakes, can even restart an exercise and generally work at a problem until they learn something new.
- *In order to learn something better, there is a need for improvement.* Improvement happens only when performance can be measured and mistakes can happen. Progress is then made by learning from the mistakes.
- *Measure progress by monitoring failed experiments.* Training in some subjects are so well established and have such long history that they can be used as an analogy when it comes to training in other subjects. Consider learning to paint. It is important for the learner to try new methods and be able to make mistakes with no ridicule, humiliation or punishment. For example, artists routinely measure progress by the number of failed experiments they go through.
- *Let learners learn from their mistakes.* To create a positive and open learning environment, allocate dedicated time so delegates can discuss their mistakes with each other and you. Ask them to share an experience where something went wrong and then explain what they have learned from it. Sharing, discussing and thinking of new potential solutions or preventions can be inspirational and incredibly useful for the whole group. In our experience at Skills Converged, almost without exception, delegates report that they learn the most through the discussion phases of a training course where they get to share their experiences with each other. In fact, a good way to think about an effective training course is that it is a structured approach in getting people to try something new, make mistakes, share their experiences in discussions and devise new methods to correct the mistakes.

> There are no mistakes, only results.

14.3 Don't Use External Rewards for Motivation

In a study on preschool children, researchers investigated the use of motivators (Lepper *et al.* 1973). They divided the children into three groups:
- *Group 1*. Researchers told Group 1 that each person would get a reward for his drawings.

- **Group 2.** For this group, researchers did not mention any rewards before the children engaged in a drawing task. However, after the drawing task was completed, the children were given an unexpected reward.
- **Group 3.** This was the control group. They were not told that they would get a reward, nor were they given any rewards after the drawing task.

A couple of weeks later, the same groups of children were put in a room for a free-play session and were provided with pens and papers for drawing. The result was that the children in Group 1 drew less than those in the other two groups.

This and similar studies in this area suggest that when external rewards are provided for a given task, people pay more attention to these rewards than to their own interest in the activity. When rewards are given for a previously unrewarded activity, people come to depend on these rewards when it comes to doing the task. If the rewards are withdrawn, interest in the activity is lost. The previous internal interest does not return, and the reward must be continuously provided to sustain interest.

In social psychology, this is known as the *overjustification effect,* and it has profound consequences. You may decide to set up a new company to provide products and services to make money. In the beginning, you might be excited about the products you are developing and the methods you use to expand your company to take a foothold in the market. Gradually, your sales start to go up, and you feel really good about making money. You may then become more and more focused on making more money, turning it into your main goal. You may start to think that cash is all that matters to the health of your company and that this is all you need to care about. As they say, cash is king. Sooner than later, there comes a year or a period in which the company takes a dive and generates less revenue and profit than before. The lost profit can then lead to the overjustification effect. You may no longer remain as interested in the company or its products and services; this is because the extrinsic reward—namely money—is gone. Once monetary incentive is withdrawn, your previous interest in producing top-quality products may not necessarily return, and this leads to disinterest, demotivation and, eventually, a failing company.

You will need to be aware of overjustification for yourself and for your delegates. If the training you provide is extrinsically motivated, you are basically there to train people for money. As soon as the money reward is affected, your interest in providing the training may decline. You can become apathetic to what learners take from the course and just turn up and go through the motions rather than been a fully engaged trainer who wants to make a difference. We have all attended such courses and we know well how they can be a complete waste of time and money.

Equally, you should also consider overjustification for your delegates. In training and education in general, overjustification happens when a learner is given extrinsic rewards to study or attend a given course. This could be in the form of scores or rankings. Once the reward is taken, the motivation to participate can disappear too. The learner may become apathetic to the course and not put much effort into it. To remedy this, you need to focus on intrinsic motivation, which means delegates need to know why they are learning something and enjoy the learning process.

14.4 Cognitive Disfluency

Consider two people who get exposed to the same information, yet one seems to learn a lot more that the other. One person sees only a stream of data—some information which is soon forgotten. The other absorbs the data, learns what it means, how to relate it to everything else, gets inspired by it and transforms the data into an *experience*. As you can imagine the latter person will have more chance of remembering and using the data than the other.

In fact, this difference is instrumental in understanding why some people are much better at learning. Equally, researchers are also interested to know what can be done to increase the efficiency of teaching.

If a delegate learns a given topic easily, the tendency is to think that the training has been successful. This is because the focus is mainly on encoding. Did the learner memorise the content? Can the learner recall the subject in a test? If the assessment is valid the trainer and the learner think that the learning activity has been successful. The problem is that what should really be evaluated is not the encoding, but instead, is how the information is retrieved and used later on. Consider the following fascinating studies.

Researchers wanted to test the effects of what is known as "cognitive disfluency." This refers to the phenomenon that people process information along a continuum from very fluently, or with great ease, to very disfluently, or with great difficulty. It has been long known that people prefer fluency over disfluency. However, recent studies show that disfluency sometimes produces outstanding results. In other words, when people learn something with more difficulty, they get to learn it better! In one study, researchers experimented with the font. The results show that by adopting a font that was slightly more difficult to read, they increased disfluency and hence increased retention and recall (Alter and Oppenheimer 2009).

In a similar study, teachers were instructed to send their training materials (worksheets and the PowerPoint slides) to researchers in advance of distributing to students (Diemand-Yauman *et al.* 2010). The researchers then changed the fonts without altering the content in any way. The new disfluent material had fonts such as Comic Sans Italicized, Monotype Corsiva, etc. which are generally harder to read. They even created disfluency by moving the paper up and down during copying process, so another kind of disfluency is created by the distortion of the materials in a way that becomes hard-to-read. The results showed that students' retention of the material across a range of topics in sciences and humanities and across several difficultly levels improved significantly when the materials was presented in a format that was harder to read.

The above studies show that the change introduced was a "desirable difficulty." This is a difficulty that is just enough to increase retention and learning performance, but not too much that puts people off the content, causes frustration and decreases motivation. It seems that influence of disfluency on retention follows a graph like this:

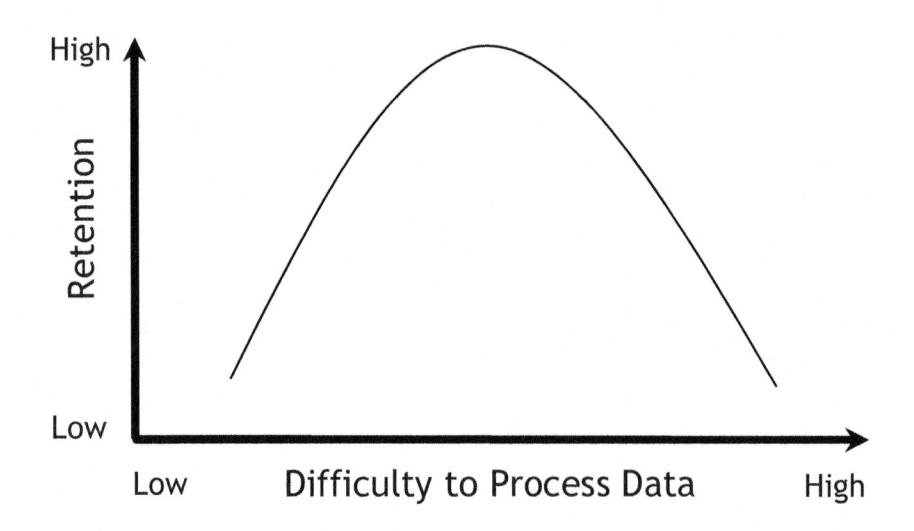

[Graph: Inverted U-curve showing Retention (Low to High) on the y-axis versus Difficulty to Process Data (Low to High) on the x-axis]

In another study, researchers from Princeton and UCLA looked at the disfluency when students took notes during lectures. Recording a lecturer's notes in longhand is more difficult and takes longer than typing on a laptop (Mueller and Oppenheimer 2014). Hence, students who use laptops spend less time actively working during lectures even though they took twice as many notes as those who wrote by hand. In other words, taking notes using a laptop is more disfluent than taking notes by hand. When the researchers examined the test scores, they found that those students who took notes by hand, scored twice as well as those who typed their notes.

On further examination, researchers wondered if this result could have been because of something else; may be the hand writers were spending more time after the class studying the materials. So they conducted another set of studies. This time, the researchers took the notes away from the students as soon as the lecture was finished and then tested them a week later. The results showed that whatever constraints were put on the group of students, those students who forced themselves to use a more disfluent method to take notes, learned more.

This shows how important it is for students to engage with the presented data to increase learning and recall. As a trainer, you should facilitate this process. The students should experiment with the data and the information they receive so they can see how it is used in practice. The process makes it more disfluent. Similarly, students should explain what they have just learned to a friend or a colleague. They should consider teaching it to a team member. Such activities will increase cognitive disfluency and thereby improve learning.

This also confirms why passively listening to a lecture will be the least disfluent method and will not have much learning value. In a training course, lecturing should be avoided as much as you can. This is also in line with many of the strategies advocated within accelerated learning. For example, interactive exercises help delegates to apply what they have just learned to a given problem. This increases disfluency. They can describe what they have learned to each other in carefully designed exercises. You will need to constantly ask questions while teaching to your delegates engaged. This forces delegates to think and hence increases disfluency. New research and your own experimentation in this area can help find new methods to make content disfluent. Remember, you only need to add enough difficulty to help boost the learning efficiency; but not too much to frustrate delegates.

Homework

Consider a course that you deliver. Analyse the course and your own behaviour by answering the following questions. You should consider going through this analysis for every course you deliver.

The course:

Is it easy for delegates to make mistakes during the course?

Do you use roleplays often that may put people on the spot?

How do you currently measure delegates' progress in a given area?

Do delegates get a chance to have a number of failed experiments during the course so they can learn from them?

Do you have sufficient number of discussions during the course to allow delegates discuss their efforts, reflect on their mistakes and share their experience with other delegates?

What is your motivation for delivering the type of courses your deliver? Answer as honestly as you can. Is there any chance that you could be extrinsically motivated and subjected to overjustification? What happens if this extrinsic motivation is removed?

How can you increase cognitive disfluency? Think of some strategies and plan a series of actions to test out your ideas. Remember, not all strategies that make a training course difficult are suitable. The aim is to find strategies that maximise learning and retention.

15 How to Be a Master Presenter

Presenting a training course is much like providing a public performance. People in your course will be looking at you more than anything or anyone else during the course. Your every move will be scrutinised by your delegates. Everything you do has a meaning for them. Delegates will be particularly observant if they are new to the subject. After all, they are there to imitate you and learn from you. You will be their role model and expert for a particular topic.

Countless observations show that trainees are particularly sensitive about training performance. If a trainer's performance is not good enough, he or she is more likely to receive poor scores at the end of the session. Delegates tend to be more forgiving about the content but fairly sensitive about performance. Sometimes, the trainer is not responsible for the content so people know that blaming the trainer would be unfair. However, if the trainer is boring, doesn't know how to teach, is difficult to understand or is not up to date with the topic, the learners will not be pleased and will voice their displeasure.

As a result, to be a successful trainer it is important that you improve your presentation skills and public performance continuously. In this chapter, you will learn about a series of guidelines that can help you improve your presentation and public performance skills.

15.1 Express Yourself Concisely

There is an art to expressing yourself in a way that makes you well understood. Fortunately, this art can be learned. All it requires is practice, persistence and self-evaluation. While presenting, always consider the following guidelines to improve the way you express yourself:

Do Not Overload the Course with Explanations

Sometimes it is tempting to go on and on about a subject. When passionate about a topic, it is easy to get carried away, but your audience may not see it this way. You may get carried away by explaining more complex topics while your audience is still pondering on what you have covered earlier.

> Describe one topic at a time and link the present topic to the next one smoothly to make it easier for learners to stay focused and absorb the information.

Be Careful with Jargons

Teaching a new skill means mentioning new jargons. Knowing jargons builds learner's confidence and increases familiarity with the field. However, be careful not to overwhelm your delegates with too many jargons. Consider repeating a new jargon several times at intervals along with its meaning before expecting delegates to learn it.

> Don't expect delegates to know what you are talking about every time you mention a new jargon if the only time you explained the jargon was at the beginning of the course.

Consider this example:

> "In the past 10 years different studies have identified that self-efficacy, locus of control, neuroticism and self-esteem are all related to each other."

If you express it like this, many people could be lost by the time you finish your sentence. They could be thinking, "What was *neuroticism* again? I know he mentioned it at some point, but I cannot remember."

Even if you have explained each jargon once at some point in the course, it is better if you describe them one more time especially now that you want to say they are all related to each other.

> Never use jargon primarily to show off your expertise. People can see through this trick very quickly and you will lose your credibility even quicker.

Connect Subjects to What They Know

Your reasoning and logic should feel familiar to your audience. Explain the new skills or content in a way that they can easily relate to.

Do Not Be Afraid to Pause

Use silence as a technique to let people ponder on what you have just said. You might have studied the field for years and even provided the training course many times in the past. You can be familiar with the content, but your learners are not. In some cases, it could be the first time that they are hearing about it. Give them time to digest it by using silence.

You can also use systematic exercises such as "interactive pause" which allow you to pause and review the new information.

Use Plenty of Examples Whenever Possible

Learning by example is usually much easier. Provide an example whenever you can to help your learners relate the topic to a practical example.

15.2 Use the Summary Sandwich Technique

When presenting or writing, always consider the following proven sequence:

> Tell them what you are going to tell them,
>
> Tell them,
>
> Tell them what you have just told them.

Sandwiching the content between two summaries in this way maximises learning. The first summary increases curiosity and allows learners to see where the new content fits. The final summary gives you a chance to recap and refresh their memory on what was just covered. This technique also helps you connect the content to the next part.

15.3 How to Avoid Making Poor Expressions

Over the years, trainers pick up some bad habits, especially when it comes to expressing themselves while explaining something. Consider the following expressions made by trainers when talking to one or more delegates:

Statement: "It is not easy…"

This negative statement is often used by trainers when a delegate is struggling with a particular skill. The trainer is trying to make the delegate feel better by reassuring him that the skill is hard to learn which is probably why the delegate is struggling. However, repeatedly saying "it's not easy" when delegates get frustrated while learning is not helpful to the learning process. This only demoralises the learners and makes the task appear unnecessarily more difficult than it is.

Statement: "Ah… It is so difficult."

Consider the following example. A trainer has just discovered that a delegate had followed a wrong procedure while going through an exercise.

The trainer wanted to explain what has gone wrong, but at the same time didn't want to get into too much detail. So he said, "Ah... it is so difficult", to which the delegate promptly replied, "Am I difficult?"

The trainer hurriedly moved on to say that this was not what he meant and that what he meant was that *explaining* this "mistake" was difficult, not that the delegate was difficult.

The problem is that there was actually nothing difficult about the explanation. It is just that the trainer wanted to explain without using too many jargons. He didn't want to confuse the delegate further and found it rather difficult to explain the issue using simpler terminology. So he said exactly how he felt.

> When someone makes a mistake, it means they are already confused and that confusion can be as a result of lack of information. Step back and explain the technique with more details, not the same level and certainly not less.

It is possible that some learners haven't understood a jargon well enough, or have forgotten about a critical step in a sequence of actions. You may not know what it is that they don't know or are confused even though you think you covered it. So you need to cover the jargons and the procedure in more detail to help them out. Do not simplify your explanation thinking that since the delegate is confused, he is not capable of learning and you must somehow reduce the amount of information. Instead, present the cases with more details, step by step and go over the explanations for any jargons you are using. Consider explaining the concept in a whole new way too.

The extra details will help their understanding and can clarify other issues that they might have Found difficult to understand.

> Never talk about the difficulty of the task or the explanation. To be safe, just don't use the word "difficult"; it does not have much use in a training environment anyway.

15.4 Body Language Plays a Critical Role in Your Training Performance

An important area in presentation skills is body language. The way you express yourself using your gestures, body posture and the tone of your voice can have a significant impact on the quality of your training.

Consider reviewing our extensive tutorial on body language available at www.SkillsConverged.com/TrainingTutorials/BodyLanguage.aspx

Homework

For this week's homework, you need to analyse your performance by observing yourself when presenting. Pick the first session of a course that you normally provide or a new course that you are planning to deliver in the future. Pick enough content that will take you half an hour to explain.

Place a camera on a tripod and capture your performance. You don't need to have anyone else in the room. This is just for your own evaluation and after recording, you can erase the video. Watching yourself can be enormously educational and despite our access to cameras in most gadgets these days few people seem to go through this highly useful exercise. Don't miss the chance to improve yourself by observing your performance. It will not only help your training delivery but also helps you improve your general personal impact.

So now feel relaxed and get into the mood of training. Assume that this is a real-world training delivery to get the best from it. Go over the following procedure to capture and analyse your training performance:

1. Plan ahead.
- A. Plan how you want to introduce yourself.
- B. Plan to start the course with a strong impression, much like a movie as you saw in the lesson on how to start a course.

2. Organise.
- A. Plan where you want to stand in the training room in relation with common objects such as your desk, laptop, screen or flipchart stand. Configure your demo room as closely as you can to this ideal training room configuration.
- B. Organise all your training resources and place them in front of you as you would in a real training room.

3. Start the video recording.

4. Start the timer and set yourself 30 minutes.

5. Start the presentation by going through the introductory part.

6. Go through the session as if you are presenting.

Train the Trainer: The Art of Training Delivery

> A. Act as if delegates are present in front of you. Ask a question and then pause as if they are answering. Continue with another question.
> B. Imagine if a delegate asks a question. Say, "Right, I see, so the question is…." and then answer it.

7. *Pay particular attention to your body language*.
   A. As you go through the self-demo, pay utmost attention to your gestures, posture and tone of voice. Aim to deliver a performance that you would be happy to watch as a delegate.

8. *Finish your performance after 30 minutes*.

9. *Review the video*.
   A. Do you introduce yourself properly? Is that what you want others to hear when they first learn about you? Does it leave a good first impression?
   B. Do you start the course in an engaging way?
   C. Do you appear confident throughout the presentation?
   D. Do you seem to know this training course by heart, as if you have delivered this course many times in the past, or do you appear new to this?
   E. Do you keep looking at your script, not knowing what to say next? Do you have a lot of pauses and "Um…" in your speech?
   F. How is your general body language? Do you appear enthusiastic or defensive? Do you appear too rigid and static, or too hyper and hence distracting?
   G. Do you use too many hand gestures or not enough?
   H. Do you keep looking at the screen or the laptop or instead do you look at the delegates, making eye contact with them?
   I. Do you turn your back to delegates while talking, especially after pointing to a screen or writing on a whiteboard or flipchart?

16 What Is the Secret in Keeping Delegates Constantly Motivated?

We have learned from previous lessons that motivated people learn better. The motivation keeps them excited about the course and the prospect of further learning. As a trainer, you need to be aware of this single parameter. As soon as delegates start to get bored or confused, the learning speed is reduced leading to more misunderstandings and a feeling that there is no need to put any effort into the process of learning.

In this chapter, we will explore an effective technique to help you keep your delegates motivated.

16.1 The Anatomy of a Course

Let's start this lesson by considering an example. A trainer is teaching a beginners course on hand building techniques using ceramics. This is a multi-day course for adults. The trainer decides to use an informal approach to training, tailored for each individual. As a result, he decides that there shouldn't be any theory and everything should be taught hands on.

Since delegates don't know much about the topic, they feel slightly lost at first but are exited enough to give it a go.

As the trainer carries on with the same informal approach, he expects each person to come up to him with questions as they arise. He would then teach each person specifically; here is how you put some *slip*, this is an *oxide* used for *glazing*, this is how you make a *slab* and so on.

As the informal approach continues, people start to get confused. Here is what might go on in their minds; how does this new information relate to what I have learned on day one? I don't know how to do this, but I feel embarrassed to constantly ask questions! I don't understand the difference between *oxidising* and *reduction*, he has never explained the difference. I know he has explained the slips before so I feel bad to ask again; he would think I am stupid.

After several sessions of unstructured teaching, there is bound to be a lot of confusion, but worse there will also be misunderstandings. It is natural for anyone who goes through a learning process to develop misunderstandings. The perception of what a person learns about a subject on day two can be quite different from what he thinks of it when the subject is revisited on day six. Later in the course, a learner understands much more about the subject but might have easily missed what was discussed at the beginning. He might have understood the concept too narrowly or even wrongly and now he needs to be corrected before moving on to more complex topics.

> The moral of the story is simple; it is correct to use *accelerated leaning principles* to engage people and teach using a hands-on experience, but it is just as important to include *structure* in the training course. Unstructured training can be slow, unmotivated and prone to bad habits or misconceptions.

This principle applies to all kinds of training courses and is not just limited to arts discussed in this example. It is just as applicable to soft skills and technical skills.

16.2 How Can You Add Structure to a Hands-on Course?

Hands-on experience and full engagement especially in art courses are still critical and must be included as part of the training methodology. So how can you add structure?

A solution is to combine two well established training methods together and oscillate between them to get the best of both worlds. Here is how it works:

1. Start with a Hands-on Approach

Sometimes, the best way to start a course is to make people familiar with a subject quickly by letting them have a go at it. This allows delegates to use all their senses, get an appreciation of the task ahead and also to understand the difficulties. This also helps you get them excited about learning the new skill.

2. Lecture to Address Developing Confusions

Once they have experienced a *taster session*, you can gather delegates together and lead them through a structured lecture or training. Your goal here is to cover theory, jargon, tool names and a little background. Your overall aim is to keep delegates excited about the topic but also to make them feel more comfortable with the domain.

Learning the jargons will help delegates communicate with you and each other more accurately. The use of jargon also boosts their confidence as they think they have learned something. Every field has a lot of jargon and familiarity with the language used in the field opens up further possibilities for people to learn as they are exposed to more content.

3. Encourage Questions

Answering questions can also indirectly clear up developing confusions for others or merely correct a misunderstanding before it is too late. Make it easy for people to ask you questions. Don't just ask, "Does anyone have any questions about anything?" You may just receive silence in return. Instead, explain something first and then expect questions related to that topic. Lead this to a discussion, so people can relate this to what they already know and ask you more questions to clarify potential confusion.

4. Get Back to Hands-on

Now that delegates know a bit more about the theory, ask them to get back and try it out. This time they will be more confident than their first attempt. Again this will motivate and energise delegates.

5. Give One More Lecture

As they develop their skills, delegates may reach a point where they would need to learn more complex tricks and techniques. A formal approach allows you to accelerate this process. Show them examples of more complex techniques used by professionals or walk through shortcuts to do something in fewer steps. Go through case studies of those who are good at this skill and analyse them. With their current understanding of the skills involved, delegates can now appreciate the work of masters on a deeper level than before. This formal step will also boost their confidence and give them an example to follow. In turn, this will excite them further and will motivate them to push forward.

6. Continue Oscillating Between Hands-on and Lecturing Approaches

From this point on, you should just oscillate between the two approaches to get the best of both worlds.

In contrast with a full hands-on approach, some trainers use the lecture format exclusively. This is of course falling off the other side. The full-time formal approach on its own can get boring very quickly. Without any engagement with tools and without involving all senses, delegates can get bored of theory and jargon and start to feel that either the content is over their head, or worse, that they don't really like this subject or domain.

A mixed approach is always the most ideal as you can easily switch between the two methods as you see fit and based on the needs of your delegates.

16.3 What to Start with: Lecture or Hands-on

In some training courses, such as teaching arts and crafts or technical skills such as learning Photoshop, you may wonder what you should start with—an introductory lecture, or an experience with tools and software.

After the introductory part, going straight to lecture can be boring. By letting delegates experience the craft or skill first, you are allowing them to get excited about the topic without going through any boring content.

This helps delegates to become familiar with the materials and tools by seeing, feeling and touching at their own individual pace.

A great approach is to start with a small task. In the ceramic course example delegates can be tasked to make a small pot. It doesn't have to be a long task, just enough to give them a taste and make them curious about the activity.

You can then continue with a short formal lecture where you describe various clay types, the tools involved and how delegates could do what they just did quicker. You can also show examples of sculptures or pots made using the same technique.

Now delegates can see that there is more to it than they first thought. Send them back for another hands-on experience and capitalise on that hidden child-like energy and curiosity.

You can apply this technique at a higher level on a multi-day course. For example, a wrong way to start a multi-day course is to only go through theory on the first day thinking that since delegates don't know anything, they need to go through a boring history and theory first and then on another day they can be introduced to tools, examples of work, etc. This is a poor approach, though it is still a common way to start in many courses, including those taught in universities or for adult learning.

A better way is to expose learners on the first day to various aspects of the skill that is fun to engage in. This taps into their natural sense of curiosity and unleashes their youthful energy to learn something new. You can then follow up by going through theory in the next session. Delegates will be more focused and engaged than they would have been having gone through it on the first day.

16.4 How to Optimise Your Training Approach

To provide a balanced training, consider the following guidelines:

People Learn Faster from Structured Information

The history and evolution of our brains can tell us a lot about our approach to handling information, in particular when our brains are overloaded.

Numerous researches in neuroscience and learning, including research carried out by Tony Buzan in 1970s, demonstrate that we learn concepts by association (Buzan 2006). When learning a new concept, we immediately want to associate it with other similar concepts we already know. It is our way of structuring information for easy recall in the future. This tendency to associate concepts together means that when trying to learn something new, we need to know where it fits. If we don't associate it with other content, it is easily forgotten.

Awareness of this concept can help you greatly in training people. When you introduce a new concept, you will need to either relate it to other content that delegates already know or create a learning environment that makes it easy for them to find these associations.

Start with the Easiest Content, then Move on to More Difficult Ones

To avoid overwhelming delegates, start with easier content first and then move on to more difficult ones. The easiest test is to see if as soon as you cover a new detailed topic, most delegates feel depressed and hopeless in ever understanding it.

If delegates think the content is way over their heads, they will switch off. There are signs to detect this feeling between your delegates. They will lose eye contact with you, start to day dream or start to chat with each other. Interestingly, they also ask fewer questions. This is a sure sign that you have gone over their limit. If people get confused or think they need clarifications, they will ask questions. However, when the content is so advanced that they don't know what it means, they simply remain quiet hoping that somehow they will learn what you are talking about.

The danger is that if they are kept in this state for too long, delegates may start thinking that either you are a bad trainer or that the subject is not useful for them. People's ego often stops them from thinking that it is their own lack of understanding or limited learning skills that could be the problem. They will blame the training course and you for it.

In any case, it is your responsibility as a trainer to make sure that the content is paced correctly and delegates are kept engaged and motivated throughout the course.

Make Them Move

When you feel that delegates are resisting to a new idea proposed to them, make them move. Research shows that when static, people are more likely to get lost in their thoughts or to hold on strongly to their position. To make them change their minds, or to unblock their minds, make them move. Remember the following fundamental principle:

> The mind follows the body and the body follows the mind.
> When people sit still, they lose the will.

The best way to make delegates move is to use an interactive exercise or an energiser that requires them to get out of their seats and move around.

Homework

Have you ever attended a course that was unstructured and fully informal? Describe it.

Analyse this course and answer the questions provided in the form below. It is always a great exercise to analyse a course you have attended yourself as a delegate. It allows you to visualise yourself in the position of a trainer without getting carried away with content. Since you probably don't know about the domain as much as the trainer, you can only focus on the training methodology. This will help you learn from other trainers' style of teaching and from potential mistakes they might be making.

If you were the trainer in the course you described above, how would you add structure to it and make it more effective?

What sequence of activities versus structured content would you use to maximise learning in this course? Provide a detailed example.

17 How to Increase the Impact of Training Using Storytelling

One of the most important tasks of a top trainer is to keep the delegates engaged. The more delegates are immersed in a training course, the more likely that they will learn. A great way to do this is to tell powerful stories. Stories capture people's imagination and help them visualise a concept.

In this chapter, you will learn why storytelling matters and how to make great stories to enhance your training.

17.1 Do Stories Matter?

How many stories do you hear in a typical day? Stories seem to be everywhere. TV is full of stories from soap operas to sitcoms to various drama series. Even news is primarily told as one story after another. Huge number of fiction and movies are consumed every single day.

Now, analyse yourself to see when you are most susceptible to persuasion. You will see that it is most often when you have been told a really good story. The story can be about anything—but it is usually a story that sells you an idea or a product.

Consider some famous public speakers. What is it about their speeches that make them stand out? It is always the story they tell us in their speeches and the way they deliver it that moves us. They make the story emotional, even somewhat personal. Their stories give us hope and promise us a better future. Their stories make us forget about the past or our everyday problems. Their stories give us energy and motivate us to follow up with an idea. There is always a protagonist to connect with emotionally. You feel their pain and joy. While the story is told, you are curious to know how it ends. You cannot wait until it reaches its climax. You want to know what the protagonist decides when he is suddenly forced to make a choice. While you are fully engaged with the story, the real message is then given to you, directly or indirectly. You understand the message through the story and you feel that you have a first-hand experience of the issue.

The real power of stories is that they can be remembered very easily and be retold to others. This is in fact largely the main way that cultural memes pass through generations.

17.2 What Can Storytelling Do for Teaching?

> When it comes to training, you have two critical aims—to teach a new skill and to increase the likelihood that this new skill is retained long after the course.

Stories can serve both needs; the story itself can be used to explain a particular concept or illustrate the benefits of following a particular attitude in a vivid way. It is also easier to remember a story which can reinforce the learning after the course. People can tell the story to others and thereby spread your training without your direct involvement.

The story can then spread by word of mouth and if it is good enough it may go viral. If it was your original story it can do wonders for your reputation as a trainer. Many people will want to know more about you and hear more stories. This is because people are addicted to good stories. We cannot get enough of them. If we discover that someone is a good storyteller and his stories work for us, we want to hear every story he has to say. We become somewhat addicted to his stories.

As a public performer who provides training courses and aspires to become more popular and better known, you cannot underestimate the power of storytelling.

17.3 The Fox, the Cat and the Wolf Have Taught Us So Much

Consider the following story.

> "Driven by hunger, a fox tried to reach some grapes hanging high on the vine but was unable to, although he leaped with all his strength. As he went away, the fox remarked, 'Oh, you aren't even ripe yet! I don't need any sour grapes.'"

What's the moral of the story? It works like this. I want something I don't have. I am certainly a capable person and deserve to have it. If I don't have it, it's because it wasn't good enough. But this leads to a conflict; either a person is capable or not. Either something is good or bad. It cannot be both. The story is about people who hold two or more conflicting ideas and firmly believe in both which leads to *cognitive dissonance*. The story vividly explains what cognitive dissonance is all about. It captures the pattern that a person desires something, finds out that it is unattainable and reduces interest in it by criticising it. Once you hear the story, it is easy to remember and it is easy to tell it to others. The story, a famous fable by Aesop and its independent variations from other cultures, provide a great way to explain a basic but powerful concept.

For example, the Persian version is like this:

> "A cat was passing the window of a neighbour's house. She saw a pan full of meat in the kitchen. Tempted to get to the meat she tried to enter through the window but he couldn't squeeze in. As she was walking away, the cat remarked, 'Oh, the meat smelled anyway.'"

This is a similar story for cognitive dissonance; just with the cat as the protagonist.

Here is another story.

> "There was a shepherd boy with a flock of sheep. Out of boredom and purely for fun he used to cry out for help, pretending that a wolf was attacking his flock. After doing this several times, the villagers realised that he was lying and stopped responding to his false cry for help. When one day the wolf really attacked the flock, the shepherd's pleas went unanswered."

The story, told countless times around the world in schools, serves to illustrate a great concept; if you lie too often no one comes to believe what you say any more. The story has become so famous that it has led to an idiomatic phrase "to cry wolf." You can teach the lesson directly, but the story is a great tool that helps to satisfy the two critical training needs identified earlier; it makes the concept *easily understood* and *memorable*.

17.4 How to Tell a Good Story

There are many different ways to make stories though good stories tend to follow a familiar proven pattern. Longer stories usually follow established forms—the kind that scriptwriters use to make movies. Shorter stories may need to skip over some parts so they can be told quickly.

Once you have selected a good story or made up your own story, you need to think about how you are going to deliver it. There is indeed an art to telling stories. We know from experience that some people are very good at it. The best way to learn about story telling is to listen to good storytellers and spot the common pattern.

Good storytelling usually has the following characteristics:

It Is Highly Engaging

A good story is often told in a dramatic way. The storyteller seems to be captivated by his own story. He is eager to tell the story, not because it makes his speech look cool, but because he *truly* thinks this is a good story, worth telling. This comes across through his body language and his tone of voice. His body language is relaxed but energetic. His tone rings with excitement.

> In short, a good story is an *experience*; make it a memorable one for your audience.

There Is a Build-up

There is usually a build-up before the main story is told. Here are some examples:

- "Let me tell you a good story I have heard from my father…"

- "Let me tell you what happened the other day when I was flying to Amsterdam…"
- "You won't believe the story I am about to tell you. Listen to this…"
- "Let me share with you a heart-breaking experience I had when talking to one of the volunteers…"
- "While I was attending a conference, a gentleman, who I didn't know at the time, came to me and told me a story that I cannot get out of my head. It changed the way I look at things and I have been thinking about it ever since. Let me share this story with you because I think everyone needs to hear about this amazing development…"

It Is Not Too Long

The longer the story, the riskier it is. The more time you spend telling the story, the more your audience expects the story to be something really interesting and useful. If the concept could be explained in two sentences there is no point to spend 5 minutes telling a wonderful story, especially if it is not that important.

> Use the following rule of thumb; does the concept you are going to explain deserve the amount of time you are going to spend telling a story about? If not, simplify your story or skip it altogether.

It Is Not Too Short

Beware of extremely short stories.

> "A man crossed a road without looking sideways because he was looking at the pretty woman on the other side. He died in the ambulance."

This story doesn't do much. It is so short there is no room to develop it. There is no point in the story where the protagonist needs to make a decision which would then lead to a climax and a consequence based on that decision. With most stories, it is this decision and the eventual consequence that teaches us something new or just entertains us. Without this decision making, you really don't have a story.

It Is Clear

A great storyteller goes through a story with just the right pace. You don't feel you are falling behind. It is delivered in clear terms and is expressed casually and somewhat informally. Slang is used in moderation, in relation with the audience and is usually included to serve a particular purpose in the story; for example, to make it funny or to indicate the class a particular character in the story belongs to.

It Is Emotional

Good stories are often emotional. A good storyteller doesn't just say, "It was snowing." He will make it a lot more emotional and personal, "It was freezing cold. I couldn't feel my toes. There was an eerie silence. Everywhere I looked it was white. I was scared I could not find my way out and I was sure I would be late for the meeting…"

> Don't just tell them a story; paint a picture.

There Is Variation in the Tone of Voice

A good storyteller's tone of voice is clear but varies as the story is told. It goes down when quoting a person who is telling a secret and it goes up when reaching a climax. It imitates an accent when talking on behalf of someone else and goes back to the narrator's accent when telling the story.

There Are One or More Pauses

A good storyteller doesn't tell a story from beginning to end in one go. He uses the story as an opportunity to tease you. He tells you the introductory part and then pauses to allow an emotional response. He then slowly continues to build up to the next climax and pauses again. Sometimes he slows the pace down by diving into more detail or background. Other times he quickly skips over details so he can get to the points that matter more.

There Is a Clear End

The end of the story comes both from the structure of the story and from the way the story is told. You can usually tell from the tone of the voice that the story is coming to an end. In contrast, a bad story finishes abruptly. You think, "Is that it?" usually followed by a thought like this, "All that for this silly punch line?"

Don't tell a story until you know it is going to be a good one, you have enough time to tell it and that you can tell it without missing a critical part.

There Is a Follow-Through

Once the story is finished, there is a pause. Either the audience laughs to the punch line or there is a reflection. Either way, the storyteller allows some time for the audience to *reflect* on the story.

In a training environment, you should lead the story to the learning points under consideration. What is the moral of the story? What would have happened if the protagonist did differently? How does the story relate to the lesson or to the audience?

17.5 Engaging Introductions

In addition to storytelling you could consider other methods to keep the delegates engaged.

Consider the following:

- *Use engaging introductions.* Just before starting each session or topic, big it up by saying how important it is. You can use dramatic titles or statements to increase curiosity.
- *Use humour.* A good training course is not just educational; it is also entertaining. Otherwise it can be very boring.

Homework

For this homework you need to make a story. Use the following instructions:

1. Pick a topic.

Pick a topic that you normally teach and that many people struggle with it. This is usually an ideal type of content to make a story about. Alternatively, pick a training course or presentation that you need to deliver in the near future. Select a topic that you can make a story about with the aim to increase the impact of the course or presentation and make it memorable. Describe the topic below.

2. Make the story.

Make or choose a story for this topic. You can make a story from scratch or adapt one to your purpose. Use the guidelines in the lesson to construct your story. Write your story below.

3. Practice delivery.

Practice telling the story several times. Now place a camera on a tripod and record yourself telling the story. Be as close as you can be to your final delivery. Record any comments below.

4. Evaluate.

Examine the video to see if you have been able to tell an engaging story. Be honest with yourself. Consider the guidelines in this lesson and score yourself on each of the following parameters between 1 and 5.

Score Sheet	
Parameter	Score (1 = Poor, 5 = Excellent)
It is highly engaging	
There is a build-up	
It is not too long	
It is not too short	
It is clear	
It is emotional	
There is variation in the tone of voice	
There are one or more pauses	
There is a clear end	
There is a follow-through	

5. Update the story and repeat.

Based on your score, change your story. Think how you could change your delivery and then tell the story to an imaginary audience in front of the camera. Evaluate as before and repeat this process until you have mastered telling the story as perfectly as you can.

6. Test it.

Tell the story to your partner or your friend—someone who is very close to you and can give you honest feedback. Take the feedback on board, update your story or the way you tell it and repeat the evaluation process.

18 Why Asking Questions Can Significantly Improve Your Training Courses

As you have seen in previous lessons, your role as a training facilitator is different from just lecturing. The aim is not to linearly provide knowledge by giving a speech; instead, you want to teach skills which are *learned* by delegates. You don't want to just raise their awareness of a topic or give them clues on where to find more information about it; in a training course you want your delegates to learn a new skill there and then. This requires participation and thinking. An important part of any effective training course is to encourage this thinking process by asking questions.

In this chapter, you will learn about the benefits of asking questions, what to ask and how to ask them.

18.1 Case Studies

Let's look at a number of common scenarios.

In a *Customer Service Skills* course:

The trainer starts by explaining the principles of customer service. He gets excited and is carried away by explaining more. Delegates meanwhile are quietly listening, feeling like they are being lectured. Fifteen minutes later, the trainer still enjoying sharing his wisdom with the class. He is unstoppable. He is now excitedly explaining various techniques. Delegates have no choice but to listen; there is no interaction between the delegates and the trainer. By now, most delegates are bored and not really absorbing much information. Many of them are looking around, paying attention to what's in the room, the decoration, what other people are wearing, etc. Gradually they all drift. Meanwhile the trainer is happy that this part is delivered so he can tick it off and move on to the next part.

In an *Illustration Skills* course:

People arrive and start to greet each other but before long the trainer cuts them off and starts the course. The trainer starts talking about various artists. He shows a few samples on a projector. There is total silence. He carries on presenting more artists and styles. Still more silence. What's happening? Are these people too shy to talk? Why is everyone so quiet? Are they paying attention? Are they interested? How would the trainer know if he is on the right track or not? Well, he has no idea, so he carries on, hoping for the best.

In a *Spanish language* course:

The trainer talks in English and explains what will happen in the course. Next, she explains a grammatical structure in English. People nod. The trainer says, "Do you know *imperative?*" Students are quiet. She explains the concept. Later, to practice vocabulary, she asks a person to read a passage. Once the passage is read, she asks, "Everyone understood?" There is silence and some nods. She says, "Good." She asks the next person to read another passage. There is a word someone doesn't know. He asks this from the tutor. The tutor explains the meaning and moves on.

Is the training working? People look bored. One person doesn't seem to understand any of it, though he doesn't ask. He is too embarrassed and doesn't want to slow down the class. After all, almost no one is asking, so he prefers to remain silent too. The trainer carries on.

In a *Microsoft Word* course:

The trainer is teaching by projecting his laptop screen on a projector. He explains how to do something in MS Word. People look and try to memorise the sequence. He carries on with another technique to explain a new method. Some people look bored. Others look totally stressed out as they cannot keep up with the complexity and options available in the software. Halfway through, they even stop taking notes. Later, they cannot remember a thing. Meanwhile, the trainer carries on explaining more techniques.

In a *Photoshop Skills* course:

The trainer explains how to carry out a particular effect. People look at the trainer's instructions on the projector and think it is fairly logical and obvious to follow the sequence. When it is their turn, they get the sequence completely mixed up. Almost no one remembers the complete sequence from memory. Delegates are baffled and somewhat embarrassed to ask. Some delegates ask the person next to them. Meanwhile, the trainer wants to get on with the next sequence and is impatiently waiting for delegates to complete their tasks. She thinks she has covered a fairly simple technique, so if they are struggling she should probably skip the more advanced content later on. After all, she has a lot to cover...

18.2 What Is Happening in all of these Training Courses?

The above situations are all familiar. Despite all the advances in training methodologies, the scenarios are still way too common. There is no doubt that these courses will not have a long lasting effect on participants. There seems to be a common pattern—that the trainers are all missing one crucial aspect of training.

Let's examine these scenarios in more detail. In the customer service skills course, delegates are lectured. Up to a point, they listen but then start to drift. There is no engagement. They don't need to listen. There is no incentive to learn—only attending the course by being physically present. The information goes through one ear and out the other. Lectures in universities and schools are followed by exams which is a strong incentive for students to pay attention and learn. If a training course, which doesn't usually have an exam, is delivered as a lecture, the chances are very high that no one will remember a thing a week later.

In the illustration skills course, the reason that people don't talk is not because they are shy; it is because they have no reason to say anything. The trainer is treating the class as a lecture and the audience, through years of conditioning in schools and universities have adopted the role of listeners sitting in a lecture. Once the audience goes into listener mode, even when asked directly, they hesitate to reply. People feel self-conscious to break the silence and the trainer has done nothing to help this or encourage them to talk.

In the Spanish Language course, the trainer is trying to engage with the audience, but she is doing it the wrong way. She is asking closed questions. When you ask the class, "Do you know X?", the most likely reply is total silence. People don't like to volunteer their lack of knowledge about something. They would rather say nothing. Those who know may just nod or be reluctant to make others feel bad about not knowing something. A closed question such as this doesn't get you anywhere. The trainer should ask open questions; "What is the meaning of X?"

Similarly, when someone asks a question about the meaning of a particular word, she doesn't have to directly answer it. Instead, she should always aim to maximise the overall engagement in the class. She could say, "Who can tell me what X means?" The trainer is now forcing others to constantly pay attention and help each other as the course progresses.

In MS Word and Photoshop training courses, the trainers are basically focused on lecturing a sequence of moves without getting the delegates to try them out.

18.3 What Is the One Thing You Need to Consider?

In all of these courses, the problem is that the trainer doesn't ask many questions and doesn't know the strength and weakness of the participants. As a trainer, if you have to get one thing absolutely right, it is that you should ask open questions all the time. You need to ask to find out what delegates know, so you can deliver at the right level. You need to ask to find out what they like to know more about and what they want to skip. You need to ask to engage. You need to ask so they don't drift. You need to ask to break the silence and encourage delegates to talk. You need to ask so they answer and hence verbalise the lessons right there and then during the course which will help their memory.

In short, remember that:

> If you don't ask, you won't know. If you don't ask, they won't learn.

Asking questions in a training course gives you the following fundamental benefits:

- *Raise interest*. Questions raise interest in a focused area.
- *Increase participation*. Questions increase participation and engagement which in turn improve memory and recall.
- *Improve thinking*. Questions improve thinking skills and the ability to think on the spot for answers. It also helps delegates to stay focused.
- *Allow assessment of knowledge*. Questions can help you assess delegates' knowledge about a certain topic. This in turn allows you to tailor the training course based on their current knowledge and specific needs.
- *Increase interaction*. Questions help to spread group knowledge. This is particularly important when teaching soft skills since a significant part of learning takes place by learning how others deal with specific situations.
- *Encourage expression*. Questions encourage expression of thoughts and feelings rather than remaining quiet and passive. This helps create a safe environment where delegates can freely talk about their problems during the course.

18.4 How to Ask Questions

Consider the following exchange between a trainer and delegates:

Trainer: "What is empathy?"

Delegate: "It is about feeling emotions."

Trainer: "Of course it is about emotions! It is kind of in the name, isn't it? Now give me another answer…"

Delegates: [Silence]

Analysis

As you can see, this is a particularly poor way of asking questions. The trainer's sarcastic remark punishes and silences everyone. No one can learn in a threatening environment. Being ridiculed in front of others will discourage people from further participation.

There is an art to asking questions. The right questions will give you all the benefits mentioned earlier; the wrong questions can offend, slow down the training, patronise and irritate the audience to the point that will stop their participation.

> Fortunately, it is easy to see if you are on the right track. Bad questions usually lead to a universal answer; *silence*.

Read silence as a cue that you need to formulate your questions differently. If people are silent, don't repeat the same question. Formulate the question in a different way to get a different result.

When asking questions consider the following guidelines:

- **Encourage a response.** Ask the question in a manner that encourages a response. Your manner should show that you accept any answer, however bad.
- **Don't ridicule.** Never ever respond sarcastically to delegates' answers. No one likes to be criticised. Your sarcastic attitude will prevent people from engaging and participating.

- *Be patient*. Once you have asked your question, pause. You know the answer usually from memory, but they need to work it out by thinking on the spot. This can take some time while the brain processes the question, finds an answer and then decides whether it is worth stating it in front of everyone else in the class. Ask a question and remain silent to allow thinking.
- *One at a time*. Don't ask multiple questions all at once. Ask one focused question and expect an answer. Then move on to the next related question, leading your audience in a particular direction.
- *Ask open questions*. Closed questions lead to a simple yes or no or a very short answer. When training others your aim is always to encourage deep thinking. Open questions are much more ideal for this purpose. Closed questions are good when you want to quickly check knowledge or decide whether covering a particular area will be useful. To ask open questions, start your question with one of the following words:

Why – Where – When – What – Who – How

- *Provide clues*. If you see that delegates are struggling with your question, provide clues to what you mean and what kind of answer you expect. Remember, your question is not a test; it is only a *tool* to encourage thinking and increase participation which would then lead to better learning and recall.
- *Engage everyone*. Some delegates are naturally quieter than others or are just too shy to answer questions. You will need to find ways to encourage everyone to participate. One way to do this is by asking targeted questions carefully. This is covered in the next section.
- *Aim questions systematically*. As a trainer you have several choices on how to aim your question. You can ask the whole group or individuals. It is important to use the correct style for what you want to achieve. Since this is an important topic, these choices are explained in more detail below.

18.5 How to Aim Questions

There are various ways to aim a question at your audience:

Group Questions

Ask the question from the whole group. Expect a volunteer to respond. This is usually the normal mode and most questions asked in a training course fall under this category.

Relay Questions

Ask a question in succession from a series of delegates. This is known as the *relay format*. Usually the question is the same and you want everyone to answer it in their own way.

Example:

"Have you ever used this particular feature of this software?"

Ask the question and then point to one person at a time, state their name, and expect them to answer the question.

ABC Questions

Suppose, you have a series of similar questions. In this case, you can ask each question directly from each delegate one at a time. It is ideal for when you want to get everyone engaged, especially those who are naturally quieter.

- *Ask*. Ask the question.
- *Break*. Pause and allow thinking.
- *Choose*. Nominate a person and ask that person to answer the question.

In practice, it is always possible that someone jumps in to answer before you choose a specific person. If this happens frequently, don't punish the person who answers by silencing him. Simply change your method to "Choose, Ask, Break" (CAB) and make it clear that you want that specific person to answer. If the person could not answer the question, you can then encourage others to volunteer.

18.6 Answering Questions

Sometimes a delegate may ask you a question. You have three main choices:

Answer Directly

You can always directly answer the question. This is ideal if you suspect that delegates are confused and you want to quickly clarify a point without introducing further confusion by more discussions.

Sometimes a delegate might be asking a question to check your expertise or only wants your specific opinion on a particular subject. The right choice is to directly answer the question.

Bounce to Others

You can bounce the question back to other delegates to answer.

Example:

> "Paul highlighted an important issue which was... Can anyone answer Paul's question?"

This method encourages participation and knowledge share which is a great way to discover how much delegates have learned so far in the course.

Bounce Back

You can bounce the question back to the person who asked it.

Example:

> "That's a good question Paul. But before I answer that, I am curious to know what you think might be the answer?

Homework

To get the best from this lesson, consider carrying out the following activities:

Task 1: Practice asking open questions. Next time you are talking to a colleague, try to only ask open questions. Set yourself a rule not to ask any closed question for the duration of your conversation.

Count the number of times you fail so you can evaluate your performance. Repeat this exercise until you are happy with your performance. Create a report of your attempts and the results you got below.

Task 2: Ask questions.

In your next training course, practice asking *Group*, *Relay*, *ABC* and *CAB* questions. Create a report of your attempts and the results you got below.

19 How to Take Advantage of the Incredible Power of Praise

Let's start this lesson by going through an example. Suppose you are running a course on customer service skills. You provide examples and case studies and expect delegates to place themselves in the position of a Customer Service Representative. You expect them to suggest what they would do or say to address specific issues.

Now imagine if all you do throughout the course is to highlight delegates' mistakes. As soon as they explain what they are going to say in a particular scenario you tell them, "But, did you know you could say something better, like this..."

If this style of training is repeated over and over again, your delegates will start to feel that they will always be *punished* for answering. The punishment is not directly negative; it is just that delegates start to feel that they never get any credit for what they get right. In other words, they are not getting enough praise.

Research shows that praising is one of the most important techniques for influencing people, in particular when it comes to learning. Nevertheless, many trainers don't seem to realise the significance of praising and the vast majority of them don't make the best of this powerful psychological technique.

In this chapter, you will learn about the benefits of giving praise and will go through a series of guidelines on how to get the most from praising in the context of training.

19.1 What Do You Gain by Praising?

Numerous studies on behavioural sciences show that most people are receptive to praise. Some psychological theories even go as far as stating that most of our actions are an attempt to win praise. There are many benefits in praising others and here is a list of critical benefits you can expect in the context of training:

- *Praise increases motivation*. People who are praised often are more motivated.
- *Praise is addictive*. Research shows that when we receive a reward that is greater than expected, a burst of Dopamine is released in the brain. Dopamine is an important neurotransmitter, responsible for a number of activities in the brain including learning. The increased Dopamine increases motivation and desire towards receiving the reward. Dopamine is a teaching signal to various parts of the brain responsible for learning new behaviour (Arias-Carrion and Poppel, 2007). So praise can be used as a reward to influence and shape behaviour while teaching.
- *Praise increases engagement*. People want to gain praise again and again (Dopamine is addictive). When you praise your delegates, they are likely to become more focused so they can be praised again. This focus might even occur unconsciously so you can capitalise on it to improve learning.
- *Praise leads to reciprocity*. When you praise people, it makes them feel good and more inclined to reciprocate. As a delegate, they may reciprocate by being more participative in the training course and become more receptive to your training methodology and expertise.

19.2 Why Don't We Praise

If praising is so good, then why don't we praise people more often? It turns out that there are a variety of reasons, some of which can have very deep roots in our behaviour and belief system. To shake up this belief system, we need to address the reasons for our behaviour.

The following are a number of such fundamental reasons. We all suffer from one or more of these beliefs to different degrees. Read each one and think about it for a minute. How much of it can you relate to?

Lack of Praise in Childhood

Cause:

> A childhood experience in which parents were reluctant to praise their children is often the reason why later on, as adults, they don't praise others enough. Some parents think that praising can affect the child's discipline and diminish his drive for achievements. This kind of belief teaches children that praise is rare and hard earned. They are not given out often or easily. Such children grow up thinking that people generally don't deserve to be praised.

How to Address:

> The first step in self-analysis is to understand this belief system. Examine how you were brought up and recall how much praise you received from your parents, teachers and other adults in your life. If you see a pattern there, then this can be part of the reason why you are not praising much now.
>
> The next step is to counteract this belief system.

Start with small praises. Just go for quantity. Even if it is a simple thank you, say it. The more you get used to praising, the faster you can get out of the old belief system.

> Once you start to become more comfortable with praise you can then deliver more specific praises and also use it in your training sessions.

Lack of Confidence

Cause:

> People who lack confidence and suffer from low self-esteem often believe that praise will elevate the status of the other person undeservedly and perhaps even at the expense of their own status and

self-worth. The feeling comes directly from the lack of confidence and from having a victim attitude.

How to Address:

Praise does not take away anything from you. Since most people are not praised enough, they desperately need it. Once they receive some praise, it is much like getting oxygen, they will *love* the person who made it happen.

In fact, most often, people view a person who praises them as someone who is strangely confident.

Consider a boss who praises his staff regularly. He will be loved for it and will be seen as a confident leader, one who is not concerned if his praises will elevate people beyond him.

The same applies to a trainer who praises his delegates every chance he gets. He is not there just to prove *he* is the expert and that delegates will never reach *his* level.

A top trainer wouldn't think that his praise will undermine his own expertise. His aim is to passionately teach a set of skills to his delegates and will use any tool—including powerful praises—to achieve it.

Don't Have Time

Cause:

A common excuse in not giving praise due to lack of time. This is usually because you think that praise should be elaborate or complex. In order to avoid doing it half-heartedly, you don't do it at all.

How to Address:

Praising doesn't take that long. As you will see in this chapter, there are a number of small steps to go through to deliver praise.

For praise to be effective, it must come at the right time. If you praise someone two weeks after the event when they have probably forgotten all about it, your praise will have very little positive effect.

Similarly, when teaching, the praise must be delivered at the time. For example, when someone gives a good answer, you have to praise them there and then. When someone finally masters a skill which he couldn't do earlier in the course, you can praise them straight away. You shouldn't wait until the end of the course to praise them all in a generic way, such as, "Yes, you all did very well." As you will see, praise is most effective when it is specific and timely.

Don't Want to Embarrass

Cause:

Another reason for lack of praising is thinking that you might somehow embarrass someone by praising them. Another related thought is that the achievement is too simple to merit a praise, so your praise may come across as patronising.

In general, if you think the risk of causing a misunderstanding is more than what you gain by praising, then you are likely not to praise.

How to Address:

The real problem here is not the size of the achievement or if the praise is seen negatively. The real problem is the method used to praise and your previous experience as a result of it.

People like to be praised, only because they are not praised enough and so when they are, it makes them feel really good about themselves. What they don't like is to receive casual meaningless praise delivered to them in a generic way—the kind that leads people to think, "You are just saying this to make me feel good, not that because I have done well."

Hence, the problem is the way that you state the praise, not the praise itself.

In a training environment, the chances are that people are constantly facing new skills. So when they achieve something, however small, it might be a big deal to them. Your own strong familiarity with a skill can distort your understanding of how your delegates feel after achieving it. You think they will be embarrassed to be praised on it because it is simple; they think they might have done fairly well and seek confirmation and encouragement to keep moving forward. They want to know if they are on the right track and you can let them know by praising. This can then motivate and encourage them to move on to more complicated tasks.

Not Impressed

Cause:

Sometimes you may think that people just don't deserve your praise. The task is too small or that the person is more capable than the task, so praising would not be right.

How to Address:

For example, suppose a learner completes a task that in your opinion is simple. You praise him by saying "Not bad, keep trying." This is not particularly positive or specific so most people will not take it as praise.

Again, bear in mind that your own familiarity with a skill can distort your view. In your eyes, a learner may not have achieved much or he hasn't achieved as much as you did when you were in his position. Understand that everyone is different and praise must be given in relation to *their* capabilities and needs, not yours or anyone else's.

Your praise must be proportional to *their* achievement. Praise is not binary; there is a spectrum and you choose the strength of the praise based on the person's specific achievement.

19.3 How to Praise in a Training Course

As you have seen earlier, there is a technique to praising. If you do it properly you will get a lot more out of it. Considering that praise is a form of influence, it is important to do it properly to maximise learning in a training environment.

To praise, use the *5-steps praise technique* as shown below. This is the generic way to praise whether in a training environment or not:

1. *Warm up.* Put it into context.
2. *Praise specifically.* The more specific you are the better.
3. *Describe the impact.* This is a critical step as it motivates the person and creates an incentive for a repeat behaviour. They need to know, from your point of view, what was the result of their activity. If you miss this step, you significantly reduce the chance of repeat behaviour as the person may not know if you approved of his or her activity.
4. *Reinforce Identity.* It shows their specific contribution and leaves no room for misunderstanding.
5. *Congratulate.* Finish off nicely.

In a training environment, you may need to skip the warm up step and get straight to the specific praise. As for reinforcing the identity, it might just be enough to mention their name unless the praise is for their specific performance in a group and you want to make sure that the praise is targeted correctly.

19.4 Guidelines on Praising in a Training Course

- *Balance repetition.* Don't exclude some delegates at the expense of others. Some people talk more often than others, especially in discussions or exercises. Be careful not to end up praising people who constantly talk while ignoring those who are quieter.
- *Balance help.* Some delegates may be slower to pick up a skill and could need more of your help. This means they could end up receiving a lot more of your praise than others just because they need a lot more attention. Make sure you explicitly praise others as well so that there is a balance.
- *Use their name.* When praising people, state their name to reinforce the identity of the person you are praising. This is particularly useful in one-day courses because it also gives you the opportunity to familiarise delegates with each other by stating their names.
- *Recall.* While you go through the course, delegates may provide good ideas and insights. Praise them at the time for their contributions. Later in the course you can recall what they have said and praise them for it again. This simple technique is particularly powerful in making people feel good about themselves and also to help them remain fully focused throughout the course. They want to win more praise which means they need to remain highly focused—precisely what you want in an ideal training environment. Here are some examples:

- o "As Mary mentioned this earlier, it is important…"
- o "Hugo spotted this pattern in scenario two…"
- o "Now at this point you can use Amir's great shortcut that he shared with us earlier…"

Homework

The homework for this chapter is fairly straight forward. The most difficult part of praising is actually doing it. How you word the praise and the delivery of it is much easier to learn.

For the homework, give praise to three people this week. They can be people you know or strangers. It is important that you fill in the following form with the details of these praises. Take it as a self-check to make sure you complete the task. It is the best way to force yourself to do it and you will be your own honest judge. Make a copy of the form and keep it with you for this week.

Person	
Name of the person you praised	
What did the person do to deserve praise?	
How did you praise this person? Provide how you expressed yourself as closely as you can remember and write it here.	

20 How to Maximise Learning by Treating Learners as Apprentices

Learning has been significantly instrumental in allowing humans to progress forward in history. Generation after generation people learn from one another. In the past, with the absence of reading materials, books and videos which we are all so used to now, people had to learn from each other through observation and imitation. Over time a whole set of principles have been developed to accelerate this process. Along with this, our understanding of learning and training has also improved significantly in recent years.

In this chapter, you will be introduced to various stages of learning and learn how to relate these stages to your training courses and maximise learning for your delegates.

20.1 How Does Learning Process Work?

By studying masters of a particular skill we can learn a lot on how skills are acquired. Historical examples of famous people such as musicians, artists, scientists, engineers, writers and craftsmen can teach us a great deal on what it takes to become really good at a new skill.

Knowing how learning works can help you in two ways. As a trainer you will be able to master the skill of training and improve your teaching style. It also helps you to understand how learning can be applied to others in your subject of teaching.

From a learner's point of view there are three stages in the learning process. These stages are applicable to all fields. As for terminology, a master is anyone who possesses the mastery of a field and is teaching or mentoring the learner (you) on it:

20.2 Stage 1: Deep Observation

Your intention here is to learn as much as possible from a master in a specific field. This is a *Passive Mode*.

To get the best from this stage, follow these rules:

- **Consider every task, no matter how menial.** Each task offers opportunities to learn something new about the skill or craft. You cannot avoid it just because you don't like it. The drudgery will focus your mind and sharpen your instincts.
- **Don't aim to get attention.** At this early stage just focus on learning about the industry, the environment and the skill.
- **Don't need to impress.** Don't focus on impressing the master or other learners. Such focus can put you on the wrong track, attract hostility from competitors and generally block your learning.
- **Be like a sponge.** Absorb as much information as you can. Consider learning the new skill as a new adventure. You need to familiarise yourself with the landscape. Where are the resources? Where are the dangers? How should you navigate the landscape? What tools do you need? Where can you get help from? What do you need to learn?
- **Show strong desire to learn, but not to outdo a master.** It is too early to think that you must surpass your master. The thought will close your eyes to reality and will prevent you from learning more.

20.3 Stage 2: Skill Acquisition

Your intention in this stage is to practice until you can acquire the skill. Your aim is to develop *tacit knowledge*. It means you can easily demonstrate the new skill in action but might find it hard to put it into words and describe how you do it.

This is much like learning cycling or driving. After an intense focused training, the knowledge required to do the task is hardwired in your brain. You no longer need to consciously think about it.

In this stage you are an *apprentice*, learning while watching and imitating. This is a *Practice Mode*.

To get the best from this stage, follow these rules:

- *Remove all distractions.* Distraction will directly interfere with the establishment of neural pathways that lead to hardwiring the brain for a particular skill.
- *Focus on one skill at a time.* Don't constantly switch between tasks and skills. You need full immersion to accelerate the process of hardwiring.
- *Take advantage of repetition.* The more you repeat the imitation, the more you learn and the easier it gets to learn. Doing something over and over again will make you aware of your strengths and weaknesses. Evaluation of your performance over time also allows you to see which areas you need to improve on.
- *Use intense focus as opposed to sporadic interest.* It is much better to spend three hours intensely focusing on one skill than to spend nine hours of unfocused attention. Your aim is to be absolutely present and immersed in the new skill.
- *Aim for real pleasure.* As you develop your skills, you become aware of the intense pleasure of achieving and overcoming challenges. Avoid short term pleasures that come from distractions and procrastination and instead aim for the joy that comes from your confidence in a new skill.

20.4 Stage 3: Experimentation

As you gain more experience in this new skill, you can now move on to an *Active Mode*. In this stage, you need to use your own initiative to apply the skill to practical applications. You start new projects, critically review other masters' works and are vocal about your views in relation to this skill.

You start to experiment in various directions to see what works and what doesn't. In this stage, you will develop your own idea of how this skill should be progressed forward. This is a smaller stage compare to the previous two although it is still as critical.

The most important rule to be aware of during this stage is that you must make the move from Skill Acquisition to this stage sooner than later. Most people take too long to do this because they are afraid. Once you know there is nothing new left to learn, make the move to Experimentation Stage. Here is a good sign to look for; when your master tells you that he is impressed with your work and your unique approach, it is probably time to move on to the Experimentation Stage.

At this stage, your work will be under constant review by the outside world and you will need to learn how to defend your views, your skills and your direction.

20.5 Why Repetition Is Fundamental to Learning

Learning anew skill can be intimidating and scary. Initially, all you see is that others who are good at this skill are far better than you.

You learn a bit, but learning can be frustrating. You need to keep repeating the learning process, but the repetition is not fun.

You might develop anxieties and even doubt whether learning the new skill is for you or you would ever be good at it.

Simply put, at this point you might not be getting much pleasure out of reviewing your own work. If you are practicing a new language, you might feel there are so many words to learn and you don't even talk as well as a child. If you are practicing painting, you think that your drawings look like children's drawings.

There is a great danger at this point that you may drop out. You just don't get as much pleasure as you thought you might when you started on this path, so you think you might as well quit.

> The solution is persistence. Carry on until you reach a *tipping point*. This is when the slight pleasure achieved through doing the task directly leads you to want to repeat it. This interest in repeating the task will in turn help you to become better at the skill, which in turn gives you more pleasure leading to more repetitions.

At this point you have entered the *cycle of accelerated returns*. As you have now developed your skill, you can start to vary it to make it more interesting and pleasurable. As you repeat more and more, the skill becomes hardwired and automatic. This in turn reduces your frustration and anxieties. You will be able to focus on higher level goals and take the skill into a whole new direction. More skills then lead to more pleasure.

20.6 How Does This Apply to Training?

Now that you know what is involved in the process of learning, let's see how this applies to training and how you, as a trainer, can use it to maximise learning. Basically, you can treat your learners as apprentices and guide them through the three stages of learning.

Consider the following techniques while you provide training:

Immerse Learners Fully

- Analyse the skills from different perspectives.
- Get learners to experience the new skills using all their senses
- Create an immersive environment. Teach the skill in an appropriate lab or a workshop related to the topic with easily accessible tools. Learners will be physically immersed and can absorb the information at their own rates.

Reduce Distractions

- Minimise any interruptions which can stop the flow.
- Don't let the delegates get interrupted by other topics. Keep the discussions and knowledge acquisition focused.
- Manage the environment so that it fully immerses delegates in a specific topic without distraction from other topics.

Cover One Topic at a Time

- This focused approach allows you to concentrate on one sub-skill at the time and make sure the training is isolated and complete.
- Minimise confusion by avoiding jumping from topic to topic. This is particularly important in discussions, so make sure delegates remain focused on the main topic.

Get Delegates to Repeat the Skill Systematically

- For the skill to become hardwired, learners need to repeat the task over and over again.
- Use memory exercises designed to enhance repeated exposure to content.

Teach Delegates the Importance of Going Through Menial Tasks

- Menial tasks help to focus the mind and provide discipline.
- The repetition provides an opportunity to increase efficiency and to do something faster and better.
- The mental discipline prepares the learners for more complex tasks ahead.

Reward for Real Achievement

- Provide prizes and reward achievements.
- Achieving is always pleasurable anyway but the prize merely reinforces the pleasure. It is basically an excuse to remind the learners that they have indeed achieved something significant and deserve a reward for their persistent efforts.

Immerse Learners by Giving Information

- During the *Deep Observation* stage, give plenty of information about the new skills. Your aim is to excite learners and help them realise the extent of the new skill. How far would they go? How would a master perform this? How extensive is the field? How is this field related to other fields? Where is the value in learning this new skill? What is the future of this field? Who are the current important players? What are the greatest discoveries, inventions or creations in this field?

Get Them to Learn—Not to Impress You

- During the *Deep Observation* stage of learning a new skill, through your manner and the way you run the course, indicate that delegates should aim to gather as much knowledge about the topic as possible and not waste time and energy trying to impress others

When They Are Ready, Encourage Them to Use Their Own Initiative

- When you see that delegates are approaching the end of *Skill Acquisition* stage, help them move up to *Experimentation Stage* by giving them a project. Your aim is to encourage delegates to use their own initiative and make decisions. These decisions would have consequences on their work and this helps them learn more from their efforts.
- Give them more elaborate coursework. Put delegates together in groups and get each group to address a particular problem. Increase the complexity of the problem or even get them to work on open problems; these are known problems that have not been addressed yet. This can excite delegates and increase their confidence. From here on, it is up to them how far they want to go and how to expand the field.

Homework

Consider your own training courses. Evaluate yourself on the guidelines that where discussed in this lesson. Do you follow them? What would you need to do for each category in order to guide your learners through the three stages of learning?

Guideline	What to do to improve on this guideline?
Immerse learners fully	
Reduce distractions	
Cover one topic at a time	
Get learners to repeat the skill systematically	
Teach learners the importance of going through menial tasks	
Reward for real achievement	
Immerse learners by giving information	
Get them to learn—not to impress you	
When they are ready, push them to use their own initiative	

21 How to Handle Group Dynamics and Create Effective Learning Groups

When running a training course you must engage the delegates in several interactive exercises. The benefits of participatory training explored in previous lessons and all research, points us towards creating an environment where people can learn from each other as well as from you, the trainer.

When running training exercises, you will inevitably end up with several groups. Usually you can set the groups yourself, but in some exercises, groups might emerge as a result of the exercise.

Either way, understanding how groups are formed and evolve can help you to manage group dynamics better and consequently provide a more effective training course.

In this chapter, you will learn about group formation and what constitutes an effective learning group.

21.1 How Groups Are Formed

People go through five predictable phases when forming a group. Each phase indicates what the group needs at that point and what issues might exist.

You can influence and guide the groups as they go through the phases. For example, depending on which phase a group is at, it could respond differently to outside change such as introduction of a new member, absence of a current member or change of objectives.

The five phases of a generic group development are as follows:

1: Beginning Phase

Characteristics:

> In this phase members seek acceptance in the group. They align themselves with other members and like to become more familiar with each other to see where everyone stands.

Role of the Trainer:

> You should encourage information exchange and create a positive learning environment where everyone feels comfortable to share their views and knowledge with others. You must also encourage those who are quieter or shyer to participate and be included in the group.

> Aim to create an atmosphere of trust. Immediately and firmly deal with ridicule or discrimination.

2: Conflict Phase

Characteristics:

> In this phase the whole group divides into subgroups. Each subgroup is formed based on similarity of members to each other (background, philosophy, etc.) or similarity of shared ideas. As a result, this can lead to conflicts of opinion. Each subgroup may set its own rules and people join different subgroups based on their beliefs or the people in that group.

Role of the trainer:

You can manage the groups to make sure the conflicts don't get out of hand. Address issues constructively and emphasise that differences of opinions are natural and expected but discrimination or rudeness is unacceptable.

3: Cohesion Phase

Characteristics:

Subgroups gradually come together as differences of opinion are resolved. There is a feeling of solidarity and the group starts to feel and act as a single entity.

Role of the trainer:

Provide support as the group goes through this phase though you must gradually adopt a hands-off approach and let the group sort its own issues. You can set challenges for the group and expect the group to respond to them. By handling the difficult challenges, the group becomes stronger.

4: Production Phase

Characteristics:

In this phase, the group goes through its peak performance. The group is now entirely focused on tasks. There is substantial co-operation and understanding between members. They know each other's strengths and weaknesses and support each other as they face bigger challenges. Members are loyal to the group and to one another.

Role of the trainer:

Since the group is at peak performance, your aim is to keep the group in this phase for as long as possible.

Your role is very small in comparison with earlier phases as the group at this point is capable of self-organisation. It should be able to resolve internal issues as they arise. You can provide more complicated challenges.

5: Conclusion Phase

Characteristics:

> All things may come to an end. In the last phase, the group must complete assigned tasks and once objectives are met it can be dissolved.
>
> In this concluding phase relationships are also dissolved. The experience can act as the seed for the next group formation and preference in selecting members.

Role of the trainer:

> This phase should not start too early. Make sure the objectives are met before the group disbands.

You can also apply these phases to the whole group of delegates attending your course. As they go through the training course, delegates will go through the five phases. Understanding and recognising these phases allow you to understand what you need to do at each stage and how to help the group to progress to the next stage.

Knowledge of group formation is also particularly useful for team building events so you can take advantage of these five phases to plan your team building training.

21.2 How to Handle Group Issues

While delegates go through various phases of group formation, the following issues may arise:

Domination

A particular problem in groups is dominant group members. If you think the group cohesion is undermined as a result of interference by one dominant member, you may need to step in to resolve the issue. Adopt the role of the leader to manage the dominating person and take control when necessary.

Withdrawal

Another problem is that a member may feel that participation in the group in not interesting anymore. Most of the time this happens because his views are not heard and others have not given him a chance to express his opinion.

Adopt the role of the leader and encourage the person to express his opinion while getting others to listen to it. Highlight this miscommunication problem to other group members and encourage equality in participation by all members so that this does not happen again.

Taking Over

Some members, especially those who are naturally dominant or over-confident may have a tendency to take over the group. This can be dominating conversations, actions or idea.

This attitude can be damaging and de-motivating for other members as they start to feel that their views are being neglected or dismissed. This can lead to apathy and withdrawal. You should step in to reduce the dominant person's influence and balance the group evenly.

21.3 Effective Learning Groups

As a trainer, your aim is to create an environment that people can easily learn new skills in it. Knowing the characteristics of an effective learning group can help you create such environment. These characteristics are as follows (Johnson and Johnson 1988):

- All members actively participate in achieving the group's objective.
- There is two-way communication between members of the group.
- There is high group cohesion.
- Group hierarchy is based on expertise, knowledge and availability and not on authority, domination or Machiavellian tactics.
- There is a great amount of mutual trust within the group.
- There are disputes and differences of opinion, though they lead to more exploration and search for optimal results than to stop it.
- Conflicts are handled by negotiation and occasionally by consulting the trainer.
- Effective interpersonal skills used by group members lead to better communication.
- There is responsibility and accountability as group members engage in various tasks.
- There is a climate of acceptance and support between members and also between members and the trainer.

Homework

The classifications on how groups go through various development phases can be quite useful and will help you manage delegates better during the course.

Consider the following scenarios and explain which development phase each group is at. Write this in the space provided.

Scenario 1:

It is the 4th day of a 5-day course. Delegates seem to be very comfortable and supportive of each other. They are eager to do more and to learn more.

Scenario 2:

The group has split into two sub-groups, each with their own strong opinion on how to proceed with the task at hand.

Scenario 3:

The group seems to be anxious and uncertain. Each person is concerned only in voicing his own views and to impress others.

Scenario 4:

It's the second day of a 3-day course and after a long debate on a change management programme recently released by the management, there is increasing agreement between the delegates on the merits of this new programme. Differences of opinion are accepted and put aside so that a single course of action can be chosen and followed.

Group development phases can also be quite useful in managing difficult situations. By analysing which phase each group is at, you can use the right strategy to deal with issues as they arise.

Consider the following scenario. Analyse it to decide which development phase the group is at and then formulate a series of strategies to handle the situation.

Scenario 5:

You have a group that consists of experts in their field. They don't seem to be participating. As discussions unfold, it seems that everyone thinks his situation is unique. You also get criticised for your generic views.

Potential solutions and strategies for the above scenarios are provided in Appendix C.

22 How to Respond if Your Training or Ideas Are Challenged

Sometimes, when delivering a training course, everything seems to go according to plan. Other times, it just doesn't seem to be working. Some delegates ask awkward questions. People look bored. The mood seems to become negative and no matter what you try it just doesn't become like the way you ran it the last time. What is going on?

In this chapter, you will learn how to handle difficult situations and what to do to avoid them all together.

22.1 You Are Wrong, I Am Right!

After you explain a concept during a course, a delegate challenges your opinion. What happens if you instantly take it as a criticism and challenge the delegate back? Other delegates are now watching in silence as they realise you have become quite emotional and defensive about the subject matter. They wonder why. In their eyes, you have become defensive and that is usually a sign that you might not be so sure of your position.

This is unfortunate since what follows is worse; you will lose your credibility and this point onwards delegates might doubt everything you say.

You can certainly discuss different aspects of an issue or concept, but enforcing a particular view just to prove delegates wrong usually means that you care more about winning an argument than teaching. This suggests that you lack confidence in an area and your giant ego cannot accept people's criticism.

22.2 How to Handle Criticism

When someone criticises you or your opinion, step back and try to see the issue from their point of view. What is the delegate trying to achieve by publicly challenging the trainer? Is he trying to make a point? Is he trying to impress you? Is he trying to show off to others? Is he trying to test you and see if you can hold your ground? Is he trying to ask a clever question just for the sake of it? Is he really challenging you or is it that you have just been sensitive about the way he has expressed his question?

People can get very emotional when they feel they are under attack. If you become emotional, it can influence your judgement therefore it is important not to handle this emotionally. This is particularly important if you are teaching a course on soft skills.

When confronted with a challenge or a criticism, immediately remind yourself that your most important aim is to maximise learning. You are the trainer and you should use this as an opportunity *to teach* and not an opportunity to impress delegates with your knowledge or personal ideas. You need to remain objective and logical, not emotional, angry, hurt or confrontational.

If you need to explore a topic from different angles and want to encourage a discussion, then that is fine so long as you do not become emotional and always consider the main objective which is to teach delegates.

In practice, there are a number of ways you can approach a criticism. These methods and their examples are explained below:

Technique 1: Gain Time

You need to give yourself enough time to think in order to approach the challenge logically and not emotionally. Buying time is a great way to calm yourself down before approaching the criticism to get best results as far as the training is concerned.

Example:

    Trainer:

"It would be great if you could explain that a little more before we explore it further."

Technique 2: Bounce

You can use the bounce technique explained in an earlier lesson on handling questions. Here, you bounce the question or challenge to other delegates and involve them in the discussion. You are stepping back to facilitate the training.

Example:

> *Trainer:*
>
> > "That is a valid remark. Class, what do you think about the concern raised by Carolyn?"

Technique 3: Reflect

You can address the presentation of the idea rather than the idea itself. You are not necessarily accepting or rejecting the idea. All you are confirming is that it is a useful topic.

Example:

> *Trainer:*
>
> > "I am glad that you brought this up. It is an interesting view worth exploring. Let me expand on the background a bit..."

Technique 4: Empathy

Sometimes, a challenge or concern is raised only to seek empathy. This is particularly the case in courses such as change management or team building where people might already have issues with the current management and see your training course as a challenge to their views. All they want is that their view is also recognised and their issues are taken on board. As a trainer, you must recognise this need and satisfy it by empathising with them.

Example:

> *Trainer:*

"I can see why you feel strongly about this. It is because [*explain what they think in your own words*]. I like to provide you a different view... [*expand on the issue*]."

22.3 What Not to Do When Challenged

Whatever method you use to address the criticism, there is one way that you must avoid:

> Do not directly challenge or ridicule the opinion of a delegate in front of the group. Never, ever, treat a challenge as a competition where you have to win to prove yourself.

The problem here is that you might win the specific argument, but as a result, will come across as defensive. Delegates will make a mental note not to argue with you as they don't want to lose the argument in front of everyone. So they simply stop challenging you, stop participating and stop listening. This will make for a bad training course. You win the battle, but lose the war!

22.4 Why People Might Be Already Thinking Negatively About the Course

Rather than waiting for challenges or difficulties to unfold, you can use a *pre-emptive* approach to minimise problems and preventing them from developing.

Before you can do this, you need to know why some people might already be feeling sceptical about your course. Sometimes people are forced by management to attend a course and are not there on their own initiative. They might already have a negative mindset before you even begin to talk. There might also be other issues such as:

- **Expecting a different trainer.** Delegates might be expecting a different trainer and instead see you in the training course. You haven't even started and they already feel disappointed.
- **Expecting a different expertise.** Delegates might already know about you and your background. They might be thinking that they

would rather have someone else who is an expert in a slightly different area or someone who, in their opinion, is better than you.
- *Expecting a different topic.* As the course unfolds, delegates can start to think that the content is not for them. They may think it is not applicable to their daily problems, is too advanced, too simple or outdated.
- *Expecting a different training venue.* Delegates might not be impressed by the training venue, its location or the refreshments.

In addition to their views about you or the course, delegates themselves may also be influenced by various personal issues that might lead them to view the course negatively. Consider these:

- *Tired.* Delegates might be tired and in general tired people are more critical.
- *Pressing deadlines.* Delegates could be preoccupied by pressing deadlines ahead and may feel attending this course at this time was not the best use of their time. Considering that courses are usually booked in advanced this is always a real possibility that you need to be prepared to handle.
- *Anxious.* Delegates might be anxious about what is going to happen during the course. This is particularly applicable if the course involves carrying out a test or a certification with a pass or fail result. Delegates can also be anxious about their own performance. For example, if the course involves roleplays or presentations it could add to delegate's anxiety level.

22.5 How to Take a Pre-Emptive Approach

The above issues lead to uncertainty, doubt and poor judgement on behalf of delegates. This can then lead to unfair criticism and negative feedbacks for you and a poor training experience for them. To avoid this, there are a number of pre-emptive approaches to minimise the occurrence or impact of these issues. Some of such steps are explained here:

Reassure Them about Your Domain Expertise

Before delegates have had a chance to develop any doubts about your expertise, demonstrate why you are the one to train them. Go over your credentials, your previous experience in the field and how extensively you are involved in training. Be careful not to brag about it. You just want to inform them about your expertise and reassure them that you are the ideal person for the job, not to rub your expertise in their faces!

Reassure Them about Your Training Expertise

People are usually inherently aware of the difference between being good at something and being good at teaching it. You can always capitalise on this. If they don't think you are the world's expert on the topic you are teaching, you can aim to reassure delegates that you are at least very good at teaching it. In most cases, people would rather be taught by a good trainer who knows the topic well than by an expert who can't teach.

Reassure Them about the Content

At the beginning of the course, you need to explain what you are going to cover in the course without going into too much detail.

After a brief summary, ask delegates to introduce themselves and state what they expect to get from the course. Connect what you are going to teach to what they want to learn. This will increase delegates' confidence in your training since they can see that it will be useful for them.

Reassure Them about the Level

Depending on the mix of delegates, this can sometimes be difficult. A great way to address this is to explain that the content has been designed for delegates with different leaning needs and expertise so that everyone will still benefit from it. You can do this through interactive exercises and discussions. At the beginning of the course however, you just want to reassure delegates that the course will be at their level.

Reassure Them about the Facilities

If something is not available in the training location, explain how an alternative is available and possibly just as good. Address any issues related to the training environment directly and early in the course before it develops into a problem. Follow the tips provided in Chapter 7 on controlling the training environment.

Make Them Excited

Excited delegates do not have time to notice any issues with the trainer or the shortcomings of the training environment. Get them excited by highlighting the cool activities that they will be participating in during the course. Get them excited about how quickly they are going to learn a new skills and how soon they will be able to put them into practice. Highlight the importance of learning the new skills and how knowing such skills will help them stand out from those who do not have the skills. Appealing to people's ego is sometimes a great motivator.

Minimise Anxiety

Address any issues that could make delegates anxious right at the beginning of the course. Do not let these anxieties distract them and affect their focus throughout the course. For example, if delegates are anxious because of a test, explain what is involved in the test or how they will have several chances at taking it.

If they need to provide a presentation, reassure delegates that it will be a short presentation and there won't be any criticism involved. Schedule the presentations at the beginning of the course so they don't have to feel anxious throughout the course and continuously worry about their presentations. Once delegates have completed the tasks, not only they would be relieved, they will also feel more confident to do it again should it be required. You should also be aware that different people react differently to workload and can experience different levels of stress.

Get Them to Forget about the Outside World

Deadlines, projects or a demanding boss can ruin a training course. Ask delegates to turn off any mobile phones and preferably don't do anything work-related during the breaks. Explain that in order for them to learn the most, they should be immersed in the training environment and keep their minds free from what is happening at work at least for the duration of the course.

Use engagement, exercises and discussions to help delegates to think about the content of the course rather than anything else. By increasing engagement, you can reduce the likelihood of daydreaming. This is why giving a lecture to an audience that is preoccupied with something else is useless.

Homework

Think about three situations in the past where you have been providing a training course and were challenged by delegates.

Question	Your Answer
What happened?	
Did you get emotional about it?	
How did you handle it?	
How would you score your performance from 1 (poor) to 5 (excellent)?	
What could you have done differently to get better results and maximise the learning for everyone in the course? Describe in detail.	

23 Training Scenarios

Delivering a good training course is an art that can be learned and mastered with practice. The secret to becoming an exceptional trainer is to reflect on your performance and to learn from them. By examining your actions and the results after delivering a training course, you can take steps to improve your training in the future.

So far, you have been introduced to a variety of guidelines on how to interact with the delegates, setup the environment and use accelerated learning principles to maximise learning. In addition to these principles, a great way to improve your training delivery is to learn from bad training examples. By examining the implications of bad training you can better understand what not to do and get rid of bad training habits.

In this chapter, you will go through a large series of examples of everyday training delivery. The examples are given in the general context of soft skills training which are easy to relate to. The principles taught here are applicable to any kind of technical training.

Main guidelines are summarised and highlighted throughout this chapter, so you can easily refer to them later to refresh your memory.

23.1 The Cascade Effect

Training delivery can be affected by many elements. One element can lead to another forming a cascade. For example, if your training materials are inadequate, the delegates need to take notes themselves which will shift their focus to something else. This in turn will tire them out which means they may not be alert enough to listen to your guidelines and training effectively. In addition, the poor quality of the training materials can reflect poorly on your expertise and delegates may come to conclude that you don't know much about the subject. One weakness can lead to another and this leads to a cascade of inefficiencies that could bring the entire training down.

As another example, if the trainer has poor mannerism, acts arrogantly and tells everyone what they should do because *he* is the expert, then people start to switch off. They may disagree with various opinions but not consider it worthwhile to show their disagreement. This in turn makes delegates more defensive and resistive to accept new ways of thinking. The training quickly becomes a waste of time and non-participation takes hold.

Hence, to deliver a good training, you must keep an eye on a variety of areas and make sure that your entire training runs smoothly. As soon as you have an area of concern, take steps to eliminate it so it doesn't cascade to other areas.

23.2 What Makes a Bad Training Session?

Most people seem to be able to recall bad training courses. These are sessions that are unforgettable for all the wrong reasons. Here are some of the main complaints reported about bad courses:

- Trainer covers a topic that delegates have zero interest in
- Lack of training materials
- Poorly designed training materials
- Not getting on with other people in the course
- Going through the training course at the wrong time
- The trainer has very poor training skills
- The trainer is an obnoxious know-it-all
- The objectives of the course are not clear

In this chapter, you will be introduced to a variety of such problems and learn to address each in order to improve the quality of your training. Most of the guidelines provided here are easy to implement. As long as you are aware of these guidelines, following them is rather easy.

23.3 Avoid Lecturing

Example:

> You want to explore the importance of leadership skills in the work place. You start by talking about the nature of leadership, then continue with a list of benefits of effective leadership and then go through an example of bad leadership. You then continue this subject by going through a better example. All of this is delivered much like a

lecture. Delegates have not said a single word throughout this part. After half an hour, you ask, "Any questions?" Delegates remain silent.

Analysis:

The example given is basically lecturing not training. You are basically talking about a subject, expecting the delegates to pick up the content as you go on. Research shows that this is a very poor method of teaching for the following reasons:

- A lecture is a one-way method of teaching—from the teacher to a learner. A lecturer cannot customise a course based on feedback because he doesn't get any feedback most of the time.
- A learner is likely to get bored and pay less attention as the lecture continues. Many people have a short attention span and a lecture does little to prevent the problems associated with this.
- A learner is not tested on the skills just taught. The lecturer assumes that the learner has learned the topic and moves on to other topics.
- The learner may misunderstand the subject but the lecturer has no way of knowing this.
- People learn at different rates. If you lecture everyone at a uniform speed, there is a risk that some people fall behind while others get bored. Research shows that this is one of the most popular reasons why university students decide not to attend a particular lecture because over time they realise that they are not really learning anything by attending the lecture that they couldn't have learned by just reading a couple of books.

How to Improve:

Rather than lecturing, train the delegates. To do this, use the following techniques:

- **Ask a lot of questions.** Instead of constantly telling delegates how something is done, ask them for their opinion and then guide them by asking more questions, helping them to find the solution themselves. Be careful not to ask questions that are way too simplistic. The aim is to keep them engaged and boost their interest in the subject matter.
- **Check understanding by testing the delegates.** After covering a topic, ask individual delegates a series of simple questions on what you have covered already and expect them to give you correct answers. This encourages the delegates to stay focused during the

training and also gives you an opportunity to see how the content has been absorbed.
- *Use plenty of interactive group exercises.* Get the delegates practice what they have learned so far. The exercises will improve recall and memorisation.

Guidelines
Ask questions rather than describe concepts in a one-way lecture
Test delegates' knowledge to make sure they have understood the content
Get delegates to participate in interactive exercises

23.4 Show How It Is Done

Example:

In a drawing class, you ask trainees to draw what they see in the object placed in front of them. Some of the trainees have never used the tools they are about to use and are somewhat new to this kind of art. They don't really know where to start, so they struggle and produce a poor result. As you walk around, you provide your specific feedback to each person but never actually show anyone how the task is done. You expect them to practice on their own and occasionally give them feedback as you go from one person to another. The trainees are left to figure it out all by themselves.

Analysis:

With no reference to how something should be done a trainee has to start from scratch and learn everything along the way. He may eventually learn, but he may have to go through many mistakes to get there. Unfortunately, this approach seems to be too common as some trainers think that they should let the trainees struggle as much as possible in order to learn. A little struggle is good but too much struggle can lead to frustration and a feeling of hopelessness. Besides, delegates may start to think that the trainer doesn't actually know much about the subject and is just facilitating them rather than training them.

Suppose you want to teach someone how to swim. You cannot teach them how to swim without actually showing a particular swimming technique. If you leave people to figure it out on their own, not only it can be quite frustrating and off putting, it can also lead to development of bad habits which you may then have to spend a lot of time to undo.

The major problem with this approach is that it is not efficient since a trainee has to make the same mistakes others have made in the past. Searching for solutions that have already been identified as poor or inadequate can waste a lot of time.

How to Improve:

A better method of teaching is to let them try first and possibly fail while aiming to help them understand the nature of the challenge. Next, as a master of the technique who is here to teach, you should demonstrate the best technique by doing it yourself in front of the learners while they watch and learn. By observing the master, they can see how something should be done correctly and then take steps to imitate the technique and eventually form their own style based on it. You can then provide customised feedback to trainees while they try to apply the technique they just observed. This way, you maximise the learning in a given time by minimising the search for methods that are already known to be substandard.

> ### Guidelines
>
> Always show the delegates how something should be done as opposed to let them find out for themselves
>
> Help delegates learn to do the task the correct way so they don't develop bad habits right from the start
>
> Let delegates have an attempt first so they can discover the magnitude of the challenge for themselves before you tell them how to tackle it

23.5 Allow Thinking Time

Example:

> You are providing a training course on time management. You ask the delegates, "What is good about using a software solution for your calendar as opposed to a paper-based calendar?" While the delegates are thinking to formulate their answer, you say, "Isn't a software solution much more dynamic and flexible to use? You can customise it much more than a paper calendar and…" You go on to describe a few more positive characteristics before stopping to see what the delegates have to say. When you stop, delegates are just nodding and remain silent.

Analysis:

> Rather than asking a question and waiting for delegates to think and state their views, you asked and carried on giving your own view of the matter straight away. This stops delegates' thinking process and makes it much more difficult for people who disagree with you to state their disagreement. They are much more likely to remain silent which means you miss an opportunity to have a useful discussion.
>
> Remember, when you ask a question, you are likely to know the answer from memory. The delegates who are new to the topic, however, need to first understand the question, relate it back to what they have learned in the course so far, formulate their answer and

finally find the courage to share their views in front of everyone else in the class. You need to allow time for this process.

How to Improve:

After asking a question, give delegates time to think about the questions you have just asked. Do not be afraid of the silence that follows. Asking questions is much easier than answering them. Allow time for people to understand the question and see where you are going with it. A bit of silence also helps those who might want to object, to go ahead with their objection. This is a great opportunity to start a discussion and see what others think.

Guidelines

Allocate time for people to formulate their answers after asking them a question

Do not ask question after question, repeatedly before delegates have had the chance to answer the earlier questions

Use silence to let delegates think and also to break the monotonic talking

23.6 Do Not Ridicule

Example:

You are training delegates on customer service skills. You ask the following question:

"A customer comes to you who is very angry about your service and somewhat aggressively says he wants to complain to the manager. What would you say?"

A delegate says:

"Angry customers are bad for business and I ask them to leave. I may even call security if they refuse to leave."

You respond:

> "That's probably the worst solution I have ever heard. I am sure someone can think of a better idea than this. Who can suggest a better response?"

This is followed by total silence as no one is brave enough to suggest anything else.

Analysis:

The trainer has punished a delegate harshly which has immediately turned the environment negative. No one likes to be told off or punished, so silence becomes the new answer as it is the safest option. In addition, because delegates cannot voice their concern, they will become defensive and resistant to new ideas and hence the training becomes a waste of time.

How to Improve:

Don't punish the delegates for making mistakes. This helps keep the learning atmosphere positive and open.

When you ask a question and the answer you get is not what you expected or is simply wrong, don't say, "That's wrong. Can anyone say what the correct answer is?" This can be punishing and humiliating and will discourage others from answering in the future. Instead, say:

> "Thanks for your suggestion, but that is not exactly what I am looking for. Can anyone else help on this?"

Or you can take this as an opportunity to initiate a discussion around the topic. Bounce it to others. For example:

> "Thanks for your suggestion. [Facing everyone else] What do you think about this response?"

If they answer wrong, don't immediately and directly correct them. Instead, say, "Why do you think this is the case? Can you give me an example for this?" To make this sound less harsh, confirm something they have said that is right and praise them for it; then move on to give the right answer.

Always praise a person who gives any answer to encourage participation. As a minimum you can always praise delegates for trying. If the answer is slightly off, you can say he is very close, but you expected something else.

Many studies show that praise is a much more effective training method than punishment. This is applicable to both adults and children. In a training environment, you should be constantly praising your delegates on their achievements—however small they may be. This may sound rather obvious and straight forward, but unfortunately, it is ignored by many trainers. Some trainers think they should only praise a delegate for exceptional performances as not to dilute or disvalue their praises. Praise is a tool that you can use to guide. It is more important to praise immediately and specifically than infrequently and generally.

Guidelines

Never ridicule a delegate's answer to your question—no matter how wrong

Never laugh at someone's wrong answer

Never allow other delegates to laugh at or ridicule other delegates' answers

Avoid using sarcastic remarks

Never ridicule a delegate as a way to teach others a lesson

Praise often when training and avoid verbal punishment or negative remarks

23.7 Don't Ask Closed Questions

Example:

You are a trainer teaching German. You ask the delegates to go through a number of sentences written in German. You ask each delegate to read one sentence from the text and then ask "Do you know what it means?" You get nods and usually a lot of silence. Once the paragraph is finished, you ask, "Everyone understands what is happening?" to which most people still nod and remain silent. You describe the meaning of a few words that you think would be helpful to explain then move on to the next paragraph and repeat with the same style of questioning.

Analysis:

When you ask closed questions about understanding you are likely to get nods and confirmations which may not represent people's true understanding of the topic. If you describe a concept and then ask, "Do you all understand?", most people will remain silent irrespective of whether they understand or not. People are reluctant to admit that they don't understand something. This is particularly the case with the adult learners.

How to Improve:

In the example above, you should ask a student to read a sentence and then state what it means in his own words. Others should remain quiet so this student is forced to come up with an answer himself.

If he failed, don't be hasty in offering the answer straight away. Praise for trying and do not say anything negative. Then you have two options:

- You can specifically ask another student to help out. You can go from student to student until someone knows the answer, or based on your own judgment you can stop and deliver the solution to accelerate the process.
- You can ask others to volunteer to help.

This way you maximise the learning by keeping everyone constantly involved even though you are asking one delegate at a time while going through the activity.

Guidelines

Ask open questions rather than closed questions

Allow the delegates to come up with solutions themselves; don't provide the answer straight away

23.8 Immerse the Delegates into the Topic Using All Their Senses

Example:

You lecture the delegates by describing the topic verbally for an extended period of time.

Analysis:

A verbal lecture is much like a speech. It is a one-way instructional method and only engages one of the senses—hearing. A speech might be suitable for a leader who wants to inspire his staff or someone who is giving a presentation in a conference about some new product. However, the speech technique is utterly unsuitable for a training environment.

Since only one sense is engaged, the human communication bandwidth is limited and you are missing on the opportunity to maximise learning.

How to Improve:

Engaging all the senses of a learner helps increase retention of the content. To do this you can use the following:

- *Appeal to sense of vision.* Research shows that we are particularly good at remembering images. This is because a large part of our brain is dedicated to image processing and image storage. You can take advantage of this remarkable ability of the human brain by using slides, images, videos and visual content during your course and increase recall.
- *Appeal to sense of touch.* Use props, puzzles, interactive exercises and so on to get the delegates use their sense of touch

while going through an exercise. This will help them remember the exercises and the content better in the future.
- *Appeal to other senses.* We use our sense of smell and taste much less often than the other three senses. However, you can still appeal to these senses where appropriate to maximise learning. For example, a chemistry teacher can easily appeal to the sense of smell. He can setup an experiment that produces a strong smell and associate the smell with the description of the process so the student can remember the process better.

Guidelines

Appeal to sense of vision by using images, slides and videos

Appeal to sense of touch by using props

Avoid the verbal, one-way speech technique. Use flipcharts and whiteboards to visualise the content as you go on so learners don't have to rely solely on their listening skills

23.9 Describe Why Something Should Be Learned

Example:

Trainer: "Right, so far we have covered how to make Gantt Charts. Now I am going to talk about CPA, or Critical Path Analysis. Basically to do CPA, you connect various work packages based on their dependency. Here, is a graph…"

Analysis:

The trainer seems to be jumping into the topic of CPA without introduction of any kind. A delegate is left to wonder where the new topic fits, why he should care about learning it and how it would relate to his work. Unfortunately, jumping into the deep end of a topic without introducing the application seems to be a common habit among trainers, teachers and lecturers. A learner who doesn't know why he should learn something can easily drift off, daydream, get bored or even resent learning the topic.

How to Improve:

When starting a new topic, go through the purpose and the application of the topic, in relation with the delegates' world. The easier the learners can see the potential relationship and benefit to their world, the more likely that they will pay attention and learn more.

In the example given above, you can say the following:

Trainer: "Right, so far we have covered how to make Gantt Charts. Now I am going to talk about a very important technique related to the analysis of Work Packages. Imagine you have a number of WPs. How would you capture their relationships? Suppose one WP is going to be delayed and you want to know how this impacts the overall project. How would you do this? How important is it to know this?... Now, there is a powerful technique known as *Critical Path Analysis* or CPA that can be used to stress test a project based on its work packages and their logical relationships. It's a very handy tool that you will be using all the time when managing projects. Has anyone heard of CPA before or is familiar with it?"

[Expect replies]

As you can see, in this example, the trainer is exploring the reasons why delegates should care to learn about CPA. By establishing the need to learn and using sentences such as, "It's a very handy tool that you will be using all the time", you gain delegates' attention and prepare the scene for an effective training.

Guidelines

Describe the importance of a topic before going into more detail

Relate the topic to the delegates' world so they can see where it fits and why they should care

Make the topic sound exciting, important and advanced to capture delegates' attention

Enquire about the subject and discover what delegates already know in order to avoid repetition

23.10 Create a Comfortable Learning Atmosphere

Example:

You are at the start of a Presentation Skills course for individuals from all walks of life. You begin the course by introducing yourself, walking through the structure of the course, talking about health and safety of the training environment and finally you move on the first session. For about half an hour into the course, the only person who has ever talked is you, the trainer. Delegates are still silent and somewhat starting to wonder if this was a good course to come to.

Analysis:

There are several issues to consider here. With this approach, the trainer doesn't know much about the delegates and their needs. He is likely to deliver a general course covering content that the delegates are already familiar with while neglecting those that delegates need to learn more about.

The other problem is that delegates don't know anything about each other and would feel like total strangers. This creates an unfamiliar atmosphere where people hesitate to talk. They may gradually warm up, but it will take a lot longer.

How to Improve:

Get people to introduce themselves to each other and familiarise themselves with everyone's names and backgrounds. By knowing what others want from the course and their backgrounds, they would feel closer to each other. This increases team bonding and helps people to listen to one another and learn from a varied set of experiences. This is particularly important when delegates are not from the same organisation and are strangers to each other. This would break the ice and make it easier for them to participate in group exercises and discussions to learn from each other.

The systematic introductions also allow you to gauge delegates' skill level in the subject and tailor the training specifically for the specific delegates you are about to train.

Guidelines

Ask delegates to introduce themselves at the beginning of the course. Encourage them to talk about their backgrounds, needs and desires in relation with the training subject

Listen to delegates' introductions and use this knowledge to customise the training course and decide which sessions you need to spend more time on or skip

23.11 Start the Course Smoothly

Example:

You have prepared your materials and got ready for the start of the course. You are sitting in one corner of the room, waiting for the delegates to arrive. The course is to start in 20 minutes. Delegates begin to arrive one by one and sit around the table. You are all sitting in awkward silence, waiting for the rest of the delegates to arrive.

Analysis:

First impression counts a lot. When delegates arrive and are confronted with total silence in a somewhat dry atmosphere, they may get the feeling that this is one of those courses they should have skipped.

How to Improve:

Create a welcoming environment at the beginning of the course to make everyone feel comfortable with each other and yourself. Simple small talks can do wonders in establishing rapport and getting people to like you. Once they like you they are more willing to listen to you and learn from you. In addition, if delegates feel they can get on well with others in the course, they will be more enthusiastic to participate in interactive exercises to learn from each as much as from the course.

You can make the environment even more positive by playing an upbeat music. There is a wide range of classical music available which are ideal for this purpose. Mozart in particular is shown to be very effective.

Guidelines

Make everyone feel comfortable as they arrive

Establish rapport with delegates and make it easy for them to establish rapport with each other

Use music to create a calming, energetic and reassuring training environment

23.12 Set a Clear Objective

Example:

You are covering SWOT analysis in a project management course. You start the session by asking the delegates, "Have you heard of SWOT analysis?" Most delegates shake their heads. You carry on as follows:

"SWOT analysis is very simple. Basically you have two dimensions like this which leads to four quarters like this. So, here you have Strengths, Weaknesses, Opportunities and Threats. Ok, now here is how you populate it…"

And you carry on explaining SWOT with an example.

Analysis:

Although you are using an example to describe the subject and walk the delegates through the technique step by step, you have missed one crucial step. What is it that the delegates are about to learn? In this example, delegates don't really know where you are going with this and they need to listen for a while before they start to understand what is going on. Besides, they don't know what they are supposed to learn by the time you have covered the topic. In other words, you have not talked about the objective of the session and instead have dived into it straight away.

How to Improve:

At the beginning of each session or when you are about to cover a new topic, state the objectives. Make sure delegates understand what they are expected to learn and what they should be able to do by the end of it. This helps them to get an idea of what you are about to cover and become more excited about learning it.

Guidelines

Always start a new session or topic by stating the general objective so delegates know what they will learn by the end of the session

23.13 Learners Should Learn on Their Own

Example:

You explain to the class that you now want to show how to create charts based on the data in a spreadsheet application. Using a projector, you start to walk through an example while delegates watch the screen. You explain and move on through a long series of steps to finish a particular example of how to carry out a particular calculation. At the end, you ask the delegates if they have any questions and then move on to the next topic.

Analysis:

Delegates are just observing. They are not engaged in the learning activity. They are very likely to get confused about the steps the trainer just explained. After all, forgetting a single step is enough to stop them from being able to create the correct chart.

How to Improve:

Learners should learn through a process of self-discovery. Watching a series of steps or reading a series of bullet points is not equivalent to learning through a hands-on experience. Get the delegates to go through the full life cycle of learning by participating in the activity. This helps them to fully appreciate the challenge and come up with relevant solutions.

For the example provided here, give delegates access to a computer and ask them to follow your steps as you go through the procedure. You also need to observe what they are doing so you can correct them if they make mistakes. Provide feedbacks there and then. Using this style of interactive learning, delegates are much more likely to remember the lessons.

Don't confuse this guide by thinking that you should let them learn on their own and not show them how something is done. It is a guided learning while you show them what to do.

Guidelines

Allow delegates to learn on their own by participating in an activity that allows them hands-on experiences and follow the technique you want them to learn

Don't limit your training to only demonstrating how something works and expecting everyone to memorise a complicated series of steps

23.14 Relate to the Learner's World

Example:

You are providing training on sales skills to a group of delegates who do most of their work on the phone and want to improve their telesales skills. As part of the general course you offer on sales skills, you go through an example of how to make a sale when visiting a client on their premises in a face-to-face meeting. The session is educational with a focus on body language, sitting arrangements, greetings and sales negotiation techniques.

Analysis:

The content you have chosen for sales skills is useful in a general sense but it is not strictly applicable to what the delegates experience as part of their daily activities. In this example, most of the delegates' activities take place on the phone. With your face-to-face example, delegates are forced to connect two different worlds and draw up their own conclusions. This puts unnecessary demand on delegates and is easy for them to miss critical points relevant to their job.

How to Improve:

The training must be relevant and related to the world of the learner rather than an abstract concept. If a learner cannot see how a technique can be applied in his daily life, the chances are that he is never going to use it.

In this example, the trainer should provide a case study when a sales activity takes place on the phone and then use the opportunity to address the critical learning points that were the intention of the original face-to-face case study.

> ## Guidelines
>
> People learn better in context as they can relate the content to their everyday tasks
>
> Provide customised examples related to the world of delegates
>
> Immerse delegates in the problem domain through relevant exercises so they can use their current domain knowledge in solving problems and immediately relate the new technique to their world.

23.15   Use Collaboration

Example:

> You need to train 20 people on how to use the latest version of a particular computer language. The plan is to choose five people for an upcoming project where this language will be used extensively. To be fair in choosing, you setup an exam at the end of the course and explain that the five individuals with the highest scores will be selected for the project. This creates a competitive environment where people feel they have to beat others in order to become part of this new exciting project. Stress levels are very high, there are some fall outs between people and very little help for each other. The selected team proves to have many problems working together and the project continuously misses deadlines while the team members blame each other for the problems.

Analysis:

> The training setup in this scenario has encouraged a competitive environment where the emphasis is on individual learning. No one likes to share what they learn with others merely because they are afraid of making it easier for others to succeed and be selected for the final project. There is a strong fear of making mistakes and there is mistrust and lack of collaboration between individuals. Some become disinterested in the subject altogether thinking there is no point to try as the chances of success are so slim.

In this case, the competitive environment is working against the learning process and is highly discouraging.

How to Improve:

Learning tends to be social. Collaboration can significantly help people learn from each other which increases the pace of learning. To create a collaborative environment, divide the delegates to small groups so they can work together while learning a new task. Encourage shared problem solving and cooperative behaviour. This increases people's interest in the subject and helps with team bonding.

Guidelines

Get delegates to collaborate with each other in solving problems

Avoid creating an atmosphere of individual competition as this reduces effective learning

Competition between groups is allowed, so long as there is collaboration among team members towards achieving a common goal

23.16 Use Many Examples

Example:

As part of a training course on handling difficult people, you make the following remark on assertiveness:

"Remember that when someone is being aggressive or difficult, you need to use assertive communication which basically means you should not be aggressive or passive. Assertiveness shows confidence and demonstrates that you have the right to your view. You don't let others to deny your rights to your view…"

You continue with the definition of the concept and eventually move on to another topic on how to handle aggressive people.

Analysis

In this scenario, the trainer is describing the concept of assertiveness in a very abstract way. This can be useful but you need to know that most people may struggle to apply such an abstract concept to everyday problems. It is one thing to know what assertiveness is, it is another to know how to use it in the right context. This is particularly important when the skill needs to be used under pressure or when someone is emotional.

How to Improve:

Use several specific examples so delegates can clearly see how a particular technique is used. Examples help delegates to learn how an abstract guideline is used in practice. Research suggests that much of learning takes place by making analogies and associations. By walking through examples, you expose delegates to a variety of situations. Having a vivid memory of such examples, it will be much easier for them to recall and apply the techniques in relevant circumstances.

Follow an example with example-driven exercises and case studies to get the delegates practice the skills during the course.

Guidelines

Use case studies and examples in your training course to help delegates relate abstract concepts to their everyday tasks

Use roleplays, examples and case studies in exercises to further immerse the delegates in the subject matter

Use simulations that put the learners in a controlled but realistic environment and help them learn the skills quickly and in context

23.17　Use Mnemonics to Help Learners Remember Sequences

Example:

You are going through a course on interview skills. In a particular session you want to explain how an interviewee should respond to a question, especially if the questions are about a behaviour taking place in the past. You explain that there are basically three steps. First you must describe the situation, then explain what you did and finally talk about your results. You give an example and then move on to another topic.

Analysis:

You have done a good job of explaining the concept and also giving an example. However, what is lacking is an easy way for the delegates to remember the technique when they need it. You should make it as easy as possible for them to remember how to respond to a question in the heat of an interview.

How to Improve:

One way to make it easier to remember the technique is to use mnemonics. This is an abbreviation of the first letters of a sequence made into a word. Remembering the word, helps you remember the series in the right order.

For the example above, you can use the following mnemonic:

- Situation or Task
- Action
- Result

The mnemonic for the technique is STAR. As you can see, the objective is to make a word out of the sequence, even if it means stretching the rule (such as using two letters for a single item).

Never use systems such as 5 P's of this and 3 A's of that. It is more difficult to remember what all the P's were than to remember a series of very different words all starting with a unique letter. Different letters also allow for sequencing in a particular order which is handy. You also don't have the problem of coming up with a bunch of really unusual words that all start with a particular letter to capture the concepts.

> ### Guidelines
>
> Take steps to help the memorisation of techniques covered in the course
>
> Use mnemonics to facilitate the memorisation of an ordered sequence of steps

23.18   Use Positive Encouragement

Example:

> You are a trainer in a drawing class. Delegates are drawing a live model. You go around observing each person's effort and provide feedback. While observing a struggling delegate you say, "It is not easy. I know. Drawing is hard. It takes years to learn."

Analysis:

> Providing individual feedback in an exercise is a great way to guide delegates. However, a negative remark such as the above example does little to help. If anything, a remark like that makes the learner feel even less confident to approach the problem. Unfortunately, many trainers repeatedly use such negative statements, as if to reassure delegates that if they are struggling, it is not because of their limited skills, but because the problem is hard. This might be true, but saying repeatedly that a particular technique is hard is a not a good strategy to help people learn.

How to Improve:

> Always praise people and use positive remarks. We can't get enough of praises. Stand out from other trainers by praising. People love being praised and would never forget those who praise them. If a task is difficult, focus on the progress a learner has made and acknowledge how quickly they have picked up the skill. Let them know how close they are in becoming an expert and how their dedication and attention to detail is helping them learn faster than others. Sometimes, it doesn't even matter if your praise is true or not, so long as it is helpful and rational. Your praise can become a self-fulfilling prophecy so don't be afraid of praising someone for something you think they don't deserve.

Guidelines

Always praise learners on what they have achieved or are about to achieve

Never glorify the difficulty of the task or make learners feel they are far away from producing good results

Think of your praise as a guidance and positive encouragement towards a specific goal as opposed to just saying they have done well

Praise the learners on their progress on the specific subject

23.19 Don't Give Generic Feedback

Example:

> You are training people on how to paint in oil. You placed a number of objects on a table so delegates can paint them as still life. You provide instructions on how to approach this task and then ask the delegates to paint what they see. As the paining is underway, you go to each person to give feedback. Most of the time you praise them on what they have done, because you don't want to put them off. In your view, none of the works are actually any good anyway. After all, this is the first time many of them are painting in oil so you cannot expect much. When giving feedback, you just want to encourage them. You don't want them to give up. You often say, "You are doing well", "I like the colours", "This is very nice" and "Very good."
>
> At the end of the course, to emphasis again, you say, "You have all done very well. I am very impressed by your work."

Analysis:

Praising is good. Encouragement can certainly be motivating, but giving feedback is not about encouragement. It is about *guidance*. In a class with many delegates, you only have limited opportunities to spend a few minutes to give feedback to each person. You must make the best of this by guiding the delegates in the right direction. You can only do this by providing specific and tailored feedback to each individual.

Generic praise is often ignored. Even more so if a delegate can hear that you are saying the same thing to everyone. Delegates will continue to do what they were doing, struggle with the task and not know if they are doing well or not.

A general praise at the end of the course for everyone may not be taken that seriously either. People may think that you say it at the end of every course so it is not really a praise for them but only a habit.

How to Improve:

You must observe behaviour, compare it with a standard you expect and then provide constructive feedback so delegates can go from where they are to where you want them to be. Any other kind of feedback would be wishy-washy generic praise.

This is why it is important to select tasks and exercises that are suitable for giving specific feedback. This is particularly a problem in art classes where people's interpretation of something can be quite subjective. How can you provide feedback on a given skill when the result is subjective? Well, you cannot—no matter how hard you try. Learning a skill is different from art critique. Objectives need to be well-defined, tasks need to be focused and skill-based and any expected progress should be measurable.

Guidelines

Give specific tailored feedback based on measured performance

Give constructive feedback. Most people learn when you tell them how they can improve on something. A general praise about the things they got right is not enough.

Don't just give a generic praise at the end of the course to everyone

23.20 Don't Criticise Harshly

Example:

>Today you are teaching your delegates about capturing light and presenting the atmosphere in your art class. You are observing a delegate who is painting a landscape and notice that she is focused on getting the details of perspective right without paying much attention to the overall lighting in the scene. In your eyes the painting doesn't look right. You tell the delegate, "I don't like this. There is no understanding of light here. It is just a bunch of stuff in a space. I don't even think you got that right. I know I am tough. When you get it right I'll tell you that it's good. If not, I tell you off. This painting is rubbish. You should start a new one."
>
>The delegate becomes upset. For the remainder of the session, she struggles to continue with the painting but she doesn't feel confident to start a new one either. Nothing seems to work for her today. She skips the next session.

Analysis:

>It is one thing to make delegates work harder, it is another to make them feel frustrated and to offend them. Learning new skills is hard. People learn at different levels and speeds. Some areas like art are mainly subjective anyway, so judging people's work is even less meaningful. There is no point to punish a delegate so harshly that the

incident becomes a negative memory on its own. You want improvement and progress, not bad memories.

How to Improve:

If you must criticise something and you think there is a potential for misunderstanding, consider using a technique known as "praise sandwich." It is rather simple and works like this:

- *Praise*. Deliver a praise for something the delegate has done well. Don't go on too much about it. You want to stay focused on the main part, but the aim here is to warm up to the criticism so you don't sound harsh.
- *Positive criticism*. Deliver your criticism in a way that can help the delegate. Positive criticism is focused on helping the delegate improve. It is not about punishment or humiliation. It is about correcting behaviour much like a parent does—with love, trust and patience.
- *Exit praise*. To reassure the delegates that you mean good, finish by praising again. Optionally, you can continue to shift to a different topic so that the whole exchange flows well.

Note that the praise sandwich works when you praise often. If you rarely praise or don't praise at all, using praise sandwich will quickly condition people on what you are doing. Each time delegates hear a praise, they expect a criticism to follow. This can become irritating and delegates would think you only praise them because you want to criticise them. If this happens, your compliment will certainly be ignored and your criticism may not be taken on board either. Ideally, you should be praising far more often than criticising so when you use a praise sandwich it would fit in with other praises.

Guidelines

Use praise sandwich to soften the delivery of your positive criticism

Praise often so that you can use praise sandwich when you need to criticise

Don't always follow a praise with a criticism or you risk devaluing your compliment

23.21   Use Balanced Discussions

Example:

> You want to increase the delegates' participation by initiating a discussion. You ask a series of open questions to kick start the discussion. A few of delegates who are very comfortable to talk in a group express their thoughts while others listen. Eventually, some of the quieter delegates try to enter the conversation by saying a few words. Their inputs are immediately expanded by the most talkative delegates. Some other delegates remain quiet for the duration of the discussions. After about 10 minutes, you ask if everyone is happy with the subject. Most people nod and you move on to the next topic.

Analysis:

> In every group you may have a few people who are talkative and dominant. A dominant talker can hijack a discussion by continuously talking and not letting anyone else talk. This can be a big problem because it can quickly bring down the quality of your training. Those who cannot get a word in feel frustrated and neglected. It is also quite possible that those who are quiet are the ones who need the training the most. As a trainer, it is your responsibility to make sure a balanced discussion takes place and no delegate dominate the discussions.

How to Improve:

> When you notice that an individual is becoming dominant, casually ask him to stop and ask others to contribute. For example, you can say:
>
>> "Thanks John, really good ideas here. Anyone else likes to expand on what we have covered so far?"
>
> If the dominant individual still dives into the conversation, look at him directly and say:
>
>> "John, I appreciate your comments on this matter. You have indeed opened up the conversation. Now, let's see what others can contribute."
>
> You can stress "others" so he gets the message. With this remark, usually people get the hint, but you still need to be observant. You don't want to be rude or aggressive towards a delegate, however, you want to let the person know politely that they need to give others a chance to participate as well. Many dominant conversationalists have a habit of talking often, so you may need to remind them of this several times.

Guidelines

It is your responsibility to make sure all delegates have a chance to contribute and no one is over shadowed by talkative extroverts

Those who are quiet might be those delegates who need the training the most. Pay particular attention to ensure they are participating

23.22   Help People to Learn from Each Other

Example:

> You are running a training course on negotiation skills. In one part of the course you go through strategies of how to bid in a negotiation. You suggest that in order to succeed you should not bid first. Bidding second will give a person a better chance of getting a favourable

position. Some delegates object. You explain the strategy again and defend it:

> "This is how you should do it. I have years of experience in the field and I can tell you from experience, this is how it is done!"

Delegates are quiet and don't look particularly convinced. You move on to other related topics. You like to think of yourself as an expert negotiator and you are here to share your expertise and experiences with this novice bunch of delegates. You don't like people challenging your ideas. You treat the training course as an event where you get to transfer *your* knowledge to others.

Analysis:

Treating training courses as a one-way information exchange is extremely limiting. Of course, it is expected that the trainer is a domain expert and knows more about the topic than the delegates. However, a trainer is not the only source of information. Delegates can also share their own experiences and insights with each other.

How to Improve:

To maximise learning in a given time, you must create an environment where delegates can learn from multiple sources. In a training session, this means learning from each other as well as from the trainer. Discussions can significantly help people to examine a subject from multiple angles. Do not assume that you are here to pass your knowledge to others. Instead, assume that you are here to facilitate the process of learning by helping delegates to look at the right content, ask the right questions and find solutions.

Guidelines

Do not treat a training course as a one-way learning activity—from you to delegates

Encourage discussions and get the delegates to share their knowledge learn as much from each other as they do from you

Get the delegates to participate in the subject so you can relate the content to their world by understanding their world view, needs and concerns

23.23 Give Meaningful Handouts

Example:

> You are preparing for the course and to make it easier for your delegates you have printed off your slides as a handout for them.

Analysis:

> Giving a copy of the slides as handouts is not very useful to delegates. You cannot put too much text in the slides and what is placed there is not often enough to refer back to.
>
> There are two critical reasons for giving handouts or workbooks in a training course. One is to minimise the time spent taking notes during the course so delegates can focus on the training instead. The other reason is for delegates to have a relatively comprehensive reference of what was covered so they can come back to it in the future to improve their skills. By giving a copy of the slides as handouts, none of these objectives are met.

How to Improve:

> Provide a bound workbook with comprehensive content organised in a way that delegates can use both during the course, as you cover various subjects, and also as a reference after the course.

Guidelines

Do not give a copy of slides as handouts

Provide a bound workbook as reference that covers all subjects discussed in the course

23.24 Be Organised

Example:

You have prepared a series of handouts to give to your delegates as you go through the course. You also have a workbook, several exercise instructions and some other forms. You have some props, a game and some playing cards. You have brought along several reference books to show to your delegates as potential further reading.

Of course, you also have your usual training equipment—your laptop, marker pens, name card, blank papers and so on.

You pile all of these on the table in front of you. As you go through the course, your search for the appropriate items to use based on what you are covering. Because you have so many things, sometimes the search takes a while and you find yourself going through many different sheets of paper before you can find what you are looking for.

At some point in the course you wonder if you have given a particular sheet to delegates, so you ask them if they have received one from you. You realise two people haven't got it so you distribute that as well.

At the end of the course you mention that you want to give them a nice handy summary of the points covered in the course, but unfortunately after a frantic search you are unable to find it and promise that you will e-mail it to them later on.

Analysis:

A person attending this course might seriously doubt the professionalism and organisational skills of the trainer. As you have seen in this example, it is quite possible that you have a lot of stuff to take with you to the course. Nothing is more critical than being organised when it comes to delivering a course. When you have to search for something, you lose precious time while all the delegates are looking at you expectantly. Under their watchful eyes, the increased pressure can make you more nervous. There is no need to bring this on to yourself.

How to Improve:

Sort everything chronologically, so you always know what to use at each stage of the course. Use the "5 Seconds" rule explained in Section 7.1.

Minimise the number of handouts by including them in a workbook or booklet. As an option, you can number the handouts, staple them together and give them to delegates at the beginning of the course. You can then simply ask everyone to use a particular form by stating its designated number.

Guidelines

Make sure you know what handouts you are giving out and when during the course

Minimise time spent hunting for appropriate handouts or instructions as it would appear unprofessional and clumsy

Aim not to give too many loose sheets to delegates during the course. Provide a bound workbook where delegates can find all the information covered in the course

23.25 Beware of Technology

Example:

You have arrived at the training venue and are setting up to start the course. You have several handouts, workbooks, exercise sheets, props and games which you need to lay out properly so they can be used efficiently in the course. You spend some time setting up the stuff. Some delegates start to arrive and you welcome them in. You move on to setup your laptop to show some slides and videos later on but realise that your laptop doesn't start. You check the cables and try again. While you are waiting nervously, other delegates arrive. You have about 5 minutes left before starting the course. You try again, and suddenly the computer turns on. You feel relieved. You smile at the delegates who are patiently sitting around the table. You hope that in a couple of minutes the system will be up and running.

Next, you connect the laptop to the projector and press the appropriate keys, but the screen doesn't come up. You are now starting to panic as everyone is looking at you while you are going through the desperate setup process. Your efforts fail so you leave the room to find someone who can help with this technical difficulty. After a few minutes you return with a technical support person who goes on to work on the laptop. At this point you can feel that the delegates are getting impatient. The slides are important to run the course and you have no other means to show them. You apologise to delegates about the delay. Some delegates start focusing on their mobile phones.

The technical support person says there is no solution and he is going to get another laptop. You decide to start the course while waiting for the new laptop to arrive. You start going through the introductions and what is going to be covered in the course. After about 10 minutes, the technical support person returns to the training room with a new laptop. He gets on with the task of setting it up and connecting it to the projector. You carry on while this is underway. Delegates are getting distracted as you try to keep the course moving while the setup is underway.

Eventually, all seems to be working. You thank the technical person and he leaves. All that is left is to open up the slides. You focus on copying the slides from the previous laptop to the new one. Delegates are now quietly watching the screen as you go through this process. After the copy is completed, you try to open your slides. An error message comes up on the screen saying that the version of the files you want to open is not supported on this laptop. People sigh.

Analysis:

This rather dramatic scenario shows how something that we take for granted can backfire with significant results. Technology is here to help us and we should make the best of it. In this case, the problem is not the technology itself that is letting us down, but what is known as *Morphy's Law*:

> If something can go wrong, it will go wrong.

It suggests that if you have to rely on several pieces of technology to get something done, make sure you have backups for these components to get the job done.

How to Improve:

Always setup your most risky equipment first. This way, if they fail, you have maximised the amount of time you have to fix your most critical components. Hence, setup your laptop and connect it to the projector before laying out your handouts, etc. as you can always do that later in case of an emergency.

Carry backup slides in printed form and possibly as overheads (if there is a device to use them) just in case. Make sure the files are universally compatible or at least convert them to a standard that you know can be read by different computers rather than only bringing files produced by the latest version of a particular software that you have on your laptop, especially if it is a fancy software that is not commonly used.

Check beforehand with the technical support of the premises to see what they can offer you in case your equipment fails. If you are using their equipment, make sure they have alternatives ready.

Guidelines

Think of backup systems for all your critical equipment and bring alternative resources as necessary

Know your equipment well so you can set them up quickly and use them with ease

Setup the riskiest equipment first

Arrive early so you have enough time to address any issues

Arrive even earlier if it is the first time you are delivering the course in this particular venue

23.26 Expand Slides Further Than What Appears in Them

Example:

> You show a number of slides with minimal content. You have been advised to include less text in your slides and you have followed suit. As you go through the course you show each slide and read from it, which is not very much. Occasionally, you ask delegates if they understood the content or if they have any questions.

Analysis:

> Reading from the slides as if they are your notes can be quite annoying for an audience. They can do the reading themselves, so what is the point of having a trainer. Along with giving a copy of the slides as handouts, this can feel like an utter waste of time for delegates since they would rather receive the slides by e-mail, speed read it and save their precious time by not attend a boring course with minimal educational value.

How to Improve:

Slides are not a place to deposit your notes. They are for delegates to look at. Use your own comprehensive notes if necessary and rehearse the course so that you know what to say for each slide. Slides are there to add extra value to what you are discussing, such as images, critical conversations, jargon, media, and so on.

Guidelines
Don't read from the slide
Don't treat the slide as a repository of your notes
Use slides as a way to expand on the content rather than mirroring what you are saying

23.27 Be Consistent on What You Cover

Example:

In your time management course, you show a slide on how to manage tasks and appointments using a software application such as Microsoft Outlook. While you are going through the slide, you show how tasks are generated. Next, you talk about the importance of minimising the number of tasks to get things done. Then you state that one way to do this is by delegating tasks. You casually move on to talk about the importance of delegation. You ask people how good they think they are at this skill. The discussions move on to various techniques uses to delegate and which style is better. After about 10 minutes, you come back to the slide to resume the discussion on creating and managing tasks in Microsoft Outlook.

Analysis:

Sometimes it can be tempting to go off on a tangent and to cover a related subject, but this is lousy training. You must keep things precise and relevant while delivering a training course. The content might be very simple to you but is usually not that simple to delegates. By covering multiple topics at once and going back and forth between them you risk confusing the delegates. It is possible that they do not learn any of it.

How to Improve:

A better approach is to cover one topic at a time. When you show a slide, only talk about the content of that slide and avoid going into other topics. You can discuss a related topic quickly but be careful not to go to deep into it. You can always say that there is time allocated for this subject later in the course and you will come back to it and that for the moment you want to focus on the current topic.

Keep your content and style of training consistent during the course so delegates know what to expect.

Guidelines
Talk about the subject shown on the slide and stay focused on the main topic
Use a consistent style so delegates know what is coming and what is expected of them

23.28 Make the Training Exciting

Example:

You need to cover risk management and probability in your Project Management course. You don't particularly enjoy this topic but this is part of the syllabus and you need to cover it regardless. You know enough about it to train others on the subject briefly and guide them to relevant sources for further study. In this course, you decide to walk through the slides quickly so you read through several slides and finish them off as soon as you can. From the delegates' point of view, you appear monotonic and boring. You are constantly looking at the slides rather than the delegates as if you don't want to give them a chance to ask questions and slow your progress.

Analysis:

Boredom is contagious. An unenthusiastic trainer can easily kill a topic. A monotone voice can put people to sleep. Any topic can be made interesting. Creative solutions not only can make the subject engaging for the delegates, but also for you.

How to Improve:

Be enthusiastic and excited about the course and the subject. Enthusiasm is contagious too. Your enthusiasm leads to an energetic delivery of the course and helps you avoid appearing monotone.

If you have a subject to go through that you find boring, think of things you can do to make it exciting, both for delegates and for yourself. In the example given, you can go through an exciting group exercise that involves probability, betting and competition. This lightens the mood and gives you an opportunity to cover the topic in a practical way rather than the dry and theoretical way. Use the following guidelines to avoid appearing monotone.

Guidelines

Periodically raise or lower your voice or vary the pitch

Occasionally move around the training room to force delegates follow you around with their eyes

Ask questions. This allows you to stop talking and break the monotone sequence.

Encourage answers so that other voices are also heard rather than only your voice

Intermittently slow down and come to a halt in your sentences to allow the delegates to fill the gap

Be enthusiastic and excited about the topic

Think of creative ways to make the content more exciting both for yourself and for your delegates

23.29   Make Slides Exciting

Example:

> You are going to show a number of slides in your course that you have prepared earlier. Each slide contains six or more bullet points. You had to use a smaller font in order to squeeze all the text in. You think it is important to have everything you want to talk about included in the slide. There are no images or visual content. You read what is written on each slide as you go through them. Delegates appear bored and non-engaged.

Analysis:

> Text is hard to read from a distance, especially if it is written in a small font. A slide is not the ideal place to deposit tons of text. Slides

should never be given as handouts so including so much text in them is unnecessary.

How to Improve:

When designing the slides, aim to increase the visual content. Images and illustrations are easier to absorb and easier to remember. A training course is not a lecture. Slides are there to help you explain a concept before you get the delegates to try it for themselves. As a result, slides cannot have much text in them. Don't design the slides as if they are your notes, helping you remember what you need to say at each stage of training. Have separate notes and write as much text in them as you want. Distribute a separate workbook and again include as much text as necessary. Once you have a good workbook and detailed notes there is little reason to have so much text in the slides.

The only exception to this rule is that if you are teaching about specific conversations. You can include the text of a conversation in one or more slides. Ideally, such conversations can be shown in a video or roleplayed but this may not always be possible or can be costly. An alternative is to place the conversation as text in the slides and read through them or better, ask a few volunteers to read them out and roleplay them.

Guidelines

Don't stuff the slides with so much text that it is difficult to read and remember

Increase the visual content. Use images, video, illustrations, demos and software in your slides

23.30 Make the Slides Informative

Example:

In contrast with the previous example, this time you decide to use purely visual content. Your slides now consist only of images. You have seen some TED presenters using these visual slides and you believe that this must be the right way to present the slides in a training course.

You talk about a particular jargon. Later, you refer back and state the jargon. Most people don't remember that you have covered it and want you to explain it again. This happens several times with various terms. You then explain a 5-step process verbally and again people have difficulty remembering the sequence later on.

Analysis:

Visual content is useful but there are certain times that text is still superior. A training course is different from a presentation. The idea is to educate people and help them learn a particular skill, not to sell an idea or a product much like TED presentations. You will need to use strategies, including showing some text in the slides, to help delegates with understanding and recall of the topic.

How to Improve:

Every time you introduce a new jargon or technical concept, it is useful to see the actual word. This helps with visualisation and avoids problems with accents. Showing the text in a slide in such cases can significantly help.

Similarly, if you covered a sequence, it is useful to show a slide that summarises the steps. This provides clarity and reduces misunderstandings. If you format the slides with minimal amount of text, the whole slide can act like a memorable image helping delegates memorise the sequence.

Guidelines

Aim to provide informative slides—not just pretty and eye-catching images

Show the text of any jargon or technical term you introduce

A training course is not a presentation; use your slides to inform and educate rather than impress and move

23.31   Get Delegates to Move Around

Example:

You have ten delegates in the training room. They are seated around a table facing you and one another. You are using a projector to show your slides. It is after lunch and you need to go through some abstract content before you get to cover more exciting examples and exercises. As you go through the subject, you notice that your delegates appear sleepy, some are yawning and others not paying much attention to you. You try to ask questions and increase participation, but there are still a lot of yawns and this starts to bother you but you don't know what else you can do.

Analysis:

Indeed, the session after the lunch is the most difficult to maintain the attention of delegates. Their digestive systems get in the way. Coupled with some abstract and boring content, this is a recipe for putting the delegates to sleep.

How to Improve:

A great way to stop delegates drifting or to get them focus more on what you are about to cover is to ask them to move.

Research shows that moving physically can lead to moving mentally. In other words, if someone is stuck in a particular state of thinking, such as daydreaming, you can shift their attention by asking them to move. This is also applicable to negotiations as well as problem solving. If you want to shift your opponent's stubborn stance on a particular issue, make them move. If somebody is stuck while solving a problem, ask them to physically move. Amazingly, some new idea may come to them. It is as if a physical move leads to a psychological move!

In the context of a training course, you can setup physical exercises to get the delegates participate in an activity that requires movement. While engaged in a physical activity, there is no way for them to daydream and you have used the potentially risky time after lunch for something useful.

You can also get the delegates to come up to the flipchart or whiteboard and write something related to the subject on it or ask a couple of people to do a quick roleplay in front of others. There are many creative solutions you can employ to keep this part of the course exciting and moving; just think of them beforehand and be prepared for this inevitable risky part of the course.

Guidelines

Ask delegates to move so they don't fall sleep or start daydreaming

Use an exercise that involves moving to prevent delegates from losing focus

Be prepared for risky parts of the courses such as after lunch and get the delegates to go through exciting content to stay engaged

23.32 Test Their Knowledge

Example:

In your project management course you want to teach the delegates how to compile Gantt Charts. You prepare your content, make some examples and bring it for delivery to the class. During the training course you walk through the content expecting everyone to learn it as you go through it. Once you have covered the content, you just move on to another topic.

Analysis:

With this style, your entire focus is on the content itself and not on the delegates. There has been no test of knowledge, no interaction and no feedback. This leads to a substandard training where success of the course largely depends on your initial intuition on how deep you need to cover each topic rather than using direct feedback from the delegates.

How to Improve:

> Training must be *learner-centred*. You must increase participation and use methods such as questions and exercises to test the delegates' knowledge and get feedback.
>
> Delegates must feel safe and accepted. This requires a positive atmosphere where everyone is encouraged to experiment without fear of rejection and ridicule. This also allows you to see how much delegates already know about the topic and how much they have learned during the course. You can then respond accordingly by spending more time on areas that delegates are weak at.

Guidelines

The focus must be on the learner, not the content

You must test delegates' knowledge on the topic before moving to another topic to ensure you are not overwhelming them

Tests and feedback allow you to see how much delegates have learned and which areas need more focus

23.33 Deliver Focused Training

Example:

> You know the importance of questions and interactions and you want to encourage discussions. When you initiate a topic you encourage the delegates to ask questions and state their views. You want to keep the conversations flowing so you don't interfere much and several delegates start their stories one after another. The topics seem to be shifting and the conversation is somewhat free flowing as everyone contributes to the mix. There are a lot of funny stories and the delegates seem to be having a good time.

Analysis:

> Engaging and humorous discussions are indeed a useful part of the training. However, it is important to guide the discussions to make sure they take place around the topic of *your* choice. It is your responsibility to make sure delegates don't go off topic.
>
> When a discussion goes off topic, the original question can be forgotten. The danger is that you can go round a circle spending a lot of time on topics that don't matter much while neglecting those that are critical to the training subject. You always have a limited amount of time and remember that at the end of the day what matters most is the training quality. This is also the way delegates will score you despite having had a good time and despite having gone off topic themselves. When the training is bad it is your fault, even if delegates cause it themselves.

How to Improve:

> Control conversations and discussions around the topic of the session. You can say:
>
>> "You all have raised very valuable points about this, but let's get back to the original question..."
>
> If it happens again, you can use a more direct command. For example, say:
>
>> "I think we are going off topic now. I really would love to carry on with this, but we don't have much time and we have a lot to cover. So I am going to ask you to consider the main question again. I want you to tell me..."

Guidelines

You are in charge of the training and it is your responsibility to make sure that the discussions do not go off topic and delegates stay focused on the training subject

23.34 Do Not Cut Off Interesting Conversations

Example:

You have planned the course and have assigned specific amounts of time for each session. In one of the sessions, you encourage a discussion around the topic of leadership. You have allocated five minutes for this part before having to move on to the next session. As the discussion unfolds, you realise that it is taking longer and many delegates seem to be very passionate about sharing their views about leadership. This goes on for a few more minutes. You think the discussion is starting to affect your schedule so you say, "Guys, we don't really have a lot of time. I am afraid we need to move on." With this, you move to the next session.

Analysis:

Cutting off a conversation which is going well may lead to several consequences. Delegates, who thought they were having a good time in the training suddenly think they could not express themselves and that the training wasn't conducted very well. It is also possible they do not feel like engaging in other conversations later on as they don't want to appear as if they are affecting your schedule. On top of this, the delegates also miss the chance to engage in a conversation which could have been a critical learning point in the course.

How to Improve:

Some conversations become the most memorable part of a course because they turn out to be novel and educational. Just because you are going off your predetermined schedule, doesn't mean you have to cut off a discussion. Allow time and re-plan the rest of the course so you can catch up.

The only exception to this rule is that when the conversation is going off-topic, in which case you need to stop, bring everyone back to the main topic, wrap up and move on.

Guidelines

Do not rush or cut off useful discussions just because you are going off your schedule

Add some contingency time before main breaks or before the end of the course. This allows you to encourage useful debate and discussions without affecting your timetable.

23.35   Minimise Visual Distractions

Example:

As you are going through the sessions you reach a point where you want to initiate a discussion between the delegates. You are facing the delegates with your back to the screen. After about ten minutes into the discussion, the screen behind you flickers and switches to screen saver mode where a piece of animation is shown. You are still engaged in the discussion and although you notice that there are a lot of glances to the screen, it doesn't register exactly what is happening.

Analysis:

It is easy to distract the audience with unnecessary visual content. Naturally, this is very unproductive and unprofessional.

How to Improve:

Make sure your laptop or projector does not switch to a screen saver mode with some distracting animation or images.

Check your training environment to make sure it does not contain moving visual content that can be distracting to delegates.

Blank the projector screen while covering content which is no longer relevant to what is shown on the slide. If you are using MS Power Point you can simply press "B" to toggle the screen on and off.

Guidelines

Switch off screen saver or any animated distracting content during the course

Turn off the screen or blank it when the slide is no longer related to the subject of discussions or exercises

Remove any visual distractions in the environment. Be particular wary of anything that moves or changes as our brains are programmed to automatically focus on moving objects.

23.36 Mix Up the Groups

Example:

> You have included several interactive exercises in the course to get the delegates practice the skills taught. Delegates are sitting around small tables which are forming several islands. You assign pairs of delegates sitting next to each other to go through an exercise together. To minimise disruptions and movement, you use the same pairs for most of the exercises throughout the course.

Analysis:

> Assigning the same people to the same groups throughout the course is not optimal. First of all, some people may not get on well with each other. By keeping them in the same group, you increase the likelihood of friction. Second, you miss on taking advantage of mindshare by getting different people to work together and learn from each other.

How to Improve:

> Setup a system where everyone gets to interact with everyone else by swapping people in groups from exercise to exercise. Consider using the *Clock Buddies Tool*[6] if you have many delegates.

---

[6] www.SkillsConverged.com/TrainingTutorials/ClockBuddies.aspx

Guidelines

If you have a few exercises swap groups after every exercise

If you have a lot of exercises, swap groups every other exercise so people in each group can go through a couple of exercises together but also get a chance to work with other people. This way, you also minimise disruptions and potential time loss due to mixing up the groups.

Change group sizes to introduce variety in exercises and in the way discussions are carried out in groups

23.37   Beware of Talkative Delegates

Example:

> While going through the course on customer service skills, you conduct several exercises and engage the delegates in a number of discussions. Mike, a senior salesman in the marketing department is one of your delegates. He has the stereotypical personality of a salesman; he talks a lot. In many of the discussions, Mike is busy expressing his views. As soon as you ask a question, Mike is first to answer it which then sets the scene for the rest of the conversation that follows. You have several delegates who remain quiet during many of these discussions purely because they cannot find a suitable gap to interject their views.
>
> Besides, Mike constantly jumps from topic to topic so before people have a chance to say something they feel it is too late as the conversation has moved on. You want to address this issue but at the same time you don't want to offend Mike or create a negative atmosphere. You feel stuck and let Mike continue talking.

Analysis:

> The problem with talkative people is that they come to dominate conversations and can easily go off-topic. As a trainer you must address this. This situation is however slightly trickier as Mike is a

senior member and although his contribution can be valuable, it is preventing others from engaging in the conversation.

How to Improve:

You have two main options here—to approach this directly or indirectly. You can directly ask Mike not to contribute for this round and let others talk. This can be rather off-putting.

Often, an indirect approach is more ideal. During discussions you can name specific people and ask them to contribute. Alternatively, you can split the group to several subgroups during discussions so that the talkative person's dominating behaviour cannot affect everyone.

Another useful indirect method is to sit next to the talkative person. This is particularly applicable to training room configurations where this is possible, such as the "Circular Formation" or "Circular Table" shown in Section 8.6 and 8.7. Not being able to have eye contact with you can reduce the urge to speak and indirectly let others to start and guide the discussions.

You may need to adjust the sitting plan between exercises or during breaks. Beware that most people are territorial and want to go back to where they first sat. You will need to break the habit by encouraging people to sit in different places so that you can sit next to the more talkative delegate.

Guidelines

Don't let talkative people dominate the conversation at the expense of those who are quieter or shy

Consider using a direct approach to ask the talkative person to remain quiet for specific periods so others can contribute too

Ask others to answer certain questions, so the talkative person cannot dominate

Divide delegates into subgroups to minimise the impact of the talkative person on all participants

Sit next to the talkative person to minimise eye contact and to discourage him from answering every question

23.38 Present to Delegates Not to the Screen

Example:

> You have a comprehensive sets of slides. You need to look at them as you explain and walk through the slides. While going through the course you look at the screen and explain the concepts.

Analysis:

> From the point of view of the audience you are facing away from them every time you look at the screen. They cannot see your lips, your voice is coming from the wrong direction and there is no eye contact. will be going off the wrong direction and there won't be any eye contact. When you lose eye contact with the audience, you miss the opportunity to get feedback from them as you explain the concepts shown on the screen. In addition, reading from the slides and constantly looking at the screen looks unprofessional.

How to Improve:

Setup your laptop/monitor in line-of-sight of the audience so you can easily look at both the audience and the screen. This prevents you from turning back or walking sideways to find out what is shown in the slide.

Use the mouse as the pointer rather than using a stick or a laser pointer so you don't have to face the screen when you want to point to something on the slide and instead can look at your laptop screen. This should make it a lot easier to look at the audience while you explain. The audience can switch between looking at you and looking at the screen with ease.

As a bonus, the mouse stays where you leave it while a stick or a laser pointer needs to be constantly controlled which means you need to constantly look at the screen. This is another reason why using a mouse is superior to using a stick or a laser pointer. For a brief pointing, where applicable, you can just use hands to point to something.

Guidelines

Make sure you maintain eye contact with your audience at all times during the course so you can receive feedback and appear more professional

Use a laptop monitor in line-of-sight of the audience

Use a mouse instead of a laser pointer or a stick

23.39 Manage Conversations

Example:

You kick start a conversation on a given topic. A few delegates excitedly talk about the subject and want to share their views. In their excitement, several people start to talk at the same time and soon you have three simultaneous conversations going on. People are taking over each other and the conversations are not related to the original question anymore.

Analysis:

In this example, you have let the conversations drift and the group to split. The result is that you lose control of what is discussed and delegates miss the opportunity to participate in all the conversations to benefit from everyone's views. It also gets very noisy, chaotic and tiring.

How to Improve:

It is your responsibility to remain in control of whatever discussions taking place during your training course. Don't allow group discussions to go into several unrelated topics. As soon as you feel this is about to happen, gain the attention of everyone by asking them to consider a specific subject. This way you force delegates to align themselves with the new topic and it usually helps everyone to come back to a single group discussion.

If you had to do this repeatedly, tell the delegates to be aware of the problem and participate in one conversation only.

There is only one exception to this general rule and that is when you specifically divide the delegates to groups, such as going through an exercise, and expect them to discuss a subject in their own specific groups.

Guidelines

Allow only one conversation at a time

You are responsible to make sure all delegates can benefit from each other's views

Encourage those that are left out of conversations to join and contribute to the single conversation

23.40   Involve Rather Than Dictate

Example:

> Throughout the course you have a tendency to explain everything. You ask very few questions. You exhibit a strong authority during the course and want to show off your expertise in the subject matter. When a few delegates object to your views, you state that you have been in this business for so long and you know how things are done and this is the way to do it. Delegates are somewhat quieter through the last parts of the course which means you end up talking almost constantly while lecturing them about the topic.

Analysis:

> This is absolutely the wrong way of delivering training. Your approach is authoritarian. Your aim is to be a facilitating trainer who is here to guide the delegates towards gaining new insights into various subjects. These insights don't necessarily have to come from you. Remember, no one will accept a radical change in their belief system because you suggested it. Instead, people must work gradually and combine what they already believe with the information. This takes time and you must allow people to find the way themselves while acting as a *facilitator* in the process.

How to Improve:

> Encourage discussions. Always deliver your training by continuously asking questions. The questioning helps delegates to think about the new information, think of what they already believe about the subject, and how these can be combined. People are much more likely to accept ideas if they feel that they have contributed to these ideas in some ways. Ask questions and guide your audience from what they know to what you want them to believe by helping them go through a path of personal discovery.

Guidelines

Do not preach or lecture

Help delegates come up with the ideas themselves

Initiate discussions by asking questions and help them view a subject from multiple angles rather than dictate a particular view

23.41 Be Engaging and Animated

Example:

You consider that training is about teaching delegates what you know about something. You just stand in the training room and cover the topics based on the specific syllabus. You are not particularly engaging. You look as if you are doing it just as another job and want to finish this course as soon as you can. You don't smile or move much and your voice is monotone. Most people attending your course find it boring, too long and not particularly useful.

Analysis:

A training course is not just about covering a syllabus. People who attend a training course are not there just to be told what to do or be made aware of something. It is more than that. They want to view a subject from a whole new angle. They are eager to get rid of their old habits, learn new skills and be excited about changing some aspect of their lives. People want to come out of a course improved in one or another. Otherwise, it is a total waste of time. In addition, what they gain should be proportional to the amount of time they spend in the course.

Delegates want to have a good time while learning something new. They love to be able to leave the course wanting to tell everybody about their experience.

How to Improve:

A presentation is much like a documentary. You want to educate and entertain at the same time. As a result, you need to be behave much like an actor. You need to be more animated and exaggerated than normal.

Use stronger gestures than you would use in a normal meeting. Use your gestures to emphasise key points. You are here to engage, entertain and educate the delegates all at once.

Think of ways to make the training a memorable experience. The more likely that the delegates remember the event, the more likely that they will remember the skills you taught them in the course.

Guidelines

Be animated and aim to engage, educate and entertain at the same time

Training courses don't need to be tough, boring and dry. Make it memorable, enjoyable and sharable

Treat a training course like a documentary; make it entertaining and informative

23.42 Manage Your Stress by Being Prepared

Example:

You have been in the company for many years and know about the customer contact database more than anyone else. As the company expert on the subject, the management has asked you to setup a training course for the rest of your colleagues. You like the challenge and have no problem with the content, but feel a bit uneasy about the training delivery. You are nervous and worried about forgetting what to say. You rehearse and rehearse again. You make a list of topics to cover and prepare some slides. Still, you are trying to remember the entire course and panic when you cannot remember a part.

Analysis:

Most people don't have photographic memories and as a trainer you don't need to rely on it either. New trainers can easily panic thinking that they need to have everything memorised as they go through the course. In practice, even experienced trainers don't need to do this. Always be aware of your stress levels and use methods to minimise your stress and make life easier for yourself.

How to Improve:

Divide the training course into a number of sessions. This is called chunking. Address each session in isolation. While going through the course, you only need to know what comes next. As a domain expert you know the content anyway. There are three critical areas you need to consider while training others:

- Know when to go through a particular topic
- Remember not to miss anything critical and cover all important areas for a given topic
- Control the pace

To satisfy all three areas, bring comprehensive notes, use slides and arrange them in a way that helps you to know what to cover next.

Have a summary of for each session and a clear objective. This is useful for delegates but also for you. Before going through each session, quickly review what you need to cover in that session. What are you trying to achieve by going through this content? How useful is this going to be for delegates based on what you currently understand of their training needs?

If your course is properly designed, you will have plenty of exercises to run. While delegates are going through some of the exercises that doesn't require your close attention, take advantage of the opportunity and review what you have covered so far and what you need to cover next.

Guidelines

Minimise your stress by being prepared and organised

Use comprehensive notes to help you remember what you need to cover at each point in the course

Just focus on remembering what comes next rather than memorising the whole content of the course

Use the time for exercises as an opportunity to review what you have covered already and what you need to cover next

23.43   Get the Timing of Your Course Right

Example:

> You have to deliver a short course on event management. You are very busy these days so you have decided to schedule the course for a slot on Friday from 1 pm to 3 pm. You expected 15 delegates. Only 9 turned up. The course is very short, so you have decided to walk through a number of screenshots to show what they need to do with the software when planning and booking an event. After about 15 minutes you start to feel that you have lost your audience and they are struggling to follow you. A few at the back are fiddling with their mobiles and a few others seem to be reading something which is not related to the course.

Analysis:

> The time slot after lunch is perhaps the worst time to setup a training course. The digestive system is in full swing and takes away a lot of our brain power. Friday as a whole is not an ideal day for training, but is practical if you are running a full day course. People finish off their work on Thursday night and focus on the training course knowing they

don't have to worry about what happens the day after. However, Friday is not an ideal day for short training courses as people are usually tired by the end of the week and training is more effective when people are fresh and awake!

In the example given above, lack of interactive content such as exercises or a chance to practice the software adds to the problem. Static delegates are much more likely to get bored, daydream or fall sleep.

How to Improve:

Run your courses on Tuesday or Wednesday. If you have a short course, run it in the morning. Monday is generally not a good day because most delegates are starting the workweek and need to deal with all the backlog of work accumulated over the weekend. There are usually many emails to process and client exchanges to go through on Mondays. In addition, people also feel that they need to warm up on Monday after the weekend break; they need to come back to the world of work. Since getting trained is a demanding activity, choose a time when most of your specific delegates are at their peak.

If you have no choice other than a time slot after lunch to deliver a short course, minimise the risk of boredom by increasing the interactivity of the training. For example, include exercises, puzzles, hands-on training, props, simulations and any useful activity that keeps them moving.

Guidelines

Run your course at a time when delegates are at their peak, without work distraction and with maximum energy

If you have to deliver at a suboptimal time, use exercises and interactive content to keep the delegates engaged and interested

Run short courses in the morning. Run day-long courses on Tuesday or Wednesday

23.44 Consider Your Delegates' State of Mind

Example:

A team of engineers have been busy for the past three months working on releasing a new product and a major prototype is due in a week. The management has noticed some conflicts within the team and wants this team to attend a team building course.

It sounded like a good idea at the time but the training didn't go as well as one hoped. Most of the discussions on how teams work ended up with people discussing their everyday issues within the team. There was a lot of blaming and finger pointing. The atmosphere became very charged and negative. People felt that the training was a waste of time. They would rather be working on the project than attending the useless course.

Analysis:

Sending staff to a training course while they have other important priorities can be a waste of time.

You also need to be careful about the sensitivity of the subject. For example, a team building course is bound to bring up a lot of discussions on how the team works. The time to go over this is not a few days before a major deadline. The team should be sent to such a course at the beginning of the project. This allows them to get to know each other more, bond, learn about each member's strengths and weaknesses and also work out a system that increases communication efficiency within the team.

How to Improve

If you have control over the timing of your training, investigate and make sure that the delegates sent to your course don't have any major deadlines due or strong priorities in the near future. Otherwise, their minds are likely to be somewhere else. If you go ahead to train people in such situations and end up with a poor training course, unfortunately it is likely that delegates would partly blame you for the lack of quality and this will not reflect well on you.

In the face of priorities, it is easy to dismiss areas of training altogether. Failure to acknowledge such matters may lead to a rebellious set of delegates who would question the need to be present in a training course or turn up reluctantly and therefore lack enthusiasm.

> ## Guidelines
>
> Consider your delegates' state of mind and arrange the training to take place when delegates don't have critical deadlines that can distract them from the training

23.45 Manage Break Times Precisely

Example:

You have finished a session and it is time for a short break. You ask the delegates to be back in about fifteen minutes. Some leave to freshen up, make calls, smoke, etc. Some remain in the room having a hot drink while chatting with others. Fifteen minutes later only 60% of delegates are present and others have not returned yet. You don't want to start the new session until everyone is back so you are impatiently waiting. You are forced to wait another ten minutes before everyone is back and you can start the session.

Analysis:

If you are supposed to have a fifteen minutes break, make sure it doesn't become 25. The lost time easily adds up in a day-long course with multiple short breaks. Staying on time shows that you are organised and allows you to provide a consistent training.

How to Improve:

Be strict in your break times. Don't say come back in fifteen minutes but instead give a precise time to be back by. For example:

> "The next session starts at 11:00. May I ask everyone to be back by then as we have a lot to cover. So please don't be late."

This illustrates that it is important to you to follow the agenda and delegates will be more likely to take it seriously too.

You can also use other incentives to get people back at a certain time. One method is to run a quiz and start it exactly at the time you want everyone to be back. Set a prize for the winner. Choose the quiz to relate to the subject of the course or the material you have already covered to benefit from the time spent on this short activity.

Guidelines

Be strict in following the agenda and show people you care about time

Provide an incentive to get people back at a certain time after a break so if they don't they feel they missed something useful or fun

Use a timer with a clear audible alarm. It helps people nearby, who might be engaged in conversations with others, to realise that they need to return.

23.46 End the Course Gracefully

Example:

You are approaching the end of the course. People can see that the time is up and the course is coming to an end so they start to pack up. As they focus on gathering their stuff and prepare to leave, you remember to mention what they need to do before coming back to the next part of the course next week. You quickly explain that you want to give them a handout and they need to answer the questions in the form. You then distribute the handout. Not many are paying attention to what you are saying. A minute later everyone is gone. You notice that some forgot to take the handouts and left it on the table.

Analysis:

For some reason we tend to be relaxed when engaged in an activity, but as soon as we realise that the time is up, suddenly the external world rushes back in and we are eager to move on to the next bit of action in our lives. A scene at the end of a course is no exception. Once people realise that the course is almost finished, they are in a rush to leave even though they have been in the course for about eight hours and a few minutes more or less shouldn't make a huge difference. This is particularly noticeable in training courses when people's external commitments can easily get in the way, and sometimes for very valid reasons. Some people may have to be somewhere else or need to catch the train home. Because of the shift in concentration at the end of a course, it is not an ideal time to go through important subjects when no one is paying much attention.

How to Improve:

The trick to have a smooth ending is not to say that the course has finished. Don't let the delegates feel that the course has ended as soon as you finish talking about the last subject. Explain that there are a few more things to go through.

Reflection at the end of any course is an important part of the session. Make sure to allocate enough time to review what has been discussed and encourage the delegates to express their views about the topics and their learnings. Creating an action plan and encouraging the delegates to commit to it is a good way of ensuring that they will use the skills learned in the course. Distribute any coursework as necessary and explain what they need to do.

Once all of these critical areas are covered, distribute feedback forms, details of follow-on courses and certificates. Once any necessary tasks are carried out declare that the course is finished and then allow delegates to leave.

Since this wrapping up at the end of the course takes time, you need to make sure you allocate time for it in your agenda. If the course is supposed to finish at 4:30, don't continue the training all the way until 4:30 before starting to wrap up. Delegates tend to get annoyed if they have to stay any longer than the given time for the end of the course. They don't see it as a generosity on your part; instead, they see it as a disorganised training. You don't want this to be the most recent image they have of the course.

Guidelines

At the end of the course, review what has been covered in the course to refresh delegates' minds

Clearly define what they need to do after the course, be it using skills, or coursework or preparation for the next part of the course

Get feedback about the course to improve on this course for future delegates

Encourage delegates to commit themselves to specific follow up actions based on what they have learned during the course

Allocate time in your agenda for wrapping up, review and feedback. This can easily take half an hour for a group of eight.

Finish the course on time to avoid disgruntled delegates

23.47 Collect Feedback in a Way That Reflects True Opinion

Example:

> At the end of the course you provide the feedback form (shown on the next page) to your delegates. This is your agency's way of evaluating trainers' performance.

COURSE EVALUATION FORM

Name: _____

Organisation: _____

Date: _____

Contact Number: _____

Email: _____

Course No.: _____

	Unsatisfactory	Satisfactory	Good	Excellent
Was the trainer				
Did you feel safe in the training environment?				
Were your needs satisfied?				
Were the refreshments				
Did the training meet your expectations?				
Were the staff behaviour				
Would you attend another course?				
Were you provided with options on which other courses you can benefit from after this course?				
Where you happy with the handouts?				

Please indicate any other concern:

Train the Trainer: The Art of Training Delivery

Analysis:

The form presented above is based on a real form used by a UK training agency. It has a number of issues and is a good example of a poorly designed form.

These are some of the problems with this form:

- The rating terms are confusing. For example, two contradictory terms such as *satisfactory* and *unsatisfactory* are used. This makes it difficult to rate between satisfactory and unsatisfactory. Something cannot be "not satisfactory" and "not unsatisfactory", but that's what it suggests if "Good" or "Excellent" are chosen.
- Questions are formulated in an inconsistent way. Generally, it is not a good idea to start a sentence and expect the name of the criteria to end it. It simply doesn't flow well.
- The questions are random and inconsistent. They ask about content, refreshments, taking other courses and then handouts.
- Generally, questions seem to be biased more for the agent as opposed to the trainer and the course content. At the end of the day, people attend the course to learn something. This must be the priority. Refreshments are important, but getting feedback about the training quality is much more critical than refreshments.
- The open question, "Please indicate any concern" focuses delegates' attention on complaining about the course rather than saying what they liked about it or providing suggestions and improvements.
- The form asks for a lot of personal information such as email address and phone number which is not really relevant when collecting feedback from delegates. Such contact details are probably already collected at the time of the booking. Make it as easy as possible for delegates to focus their energy on giving you feedback, rather than deciding what kind of personal information they can disclose.
- The form is distributed and collected by the trainer. Normally people wouldn't feel comfortable making negative remarks on the form that clearly identifies who they are. Refer to a number of solutions suggested for this in Section 4.10.

How to Improve:

Use a consistent rating such as 1 to 5 representing *Bad* to *Excellent*. Now it is simple to measure. You can also choose 1 to 4 so there is no middle score and people are forced to vote positively or negatively about each question.

Formulate questions in a consistent way without including the criteria in the question.

Divide the questions into a series of categories, such as Content, Delivery and Facilities where each section contains a short number of critical questions related to that area.

For open questions ask in a way to get useful answers. Here are some suggestions:

- What did you like the most about the course?
- What did you like the least about the course?
- What was the most important lesson you learned today?
- If you had to choose one area that we could improve on, what would it be?
- Which topic impressed you the most?

Guidelines

Use a well-designed feedback form that encourages delegates to tell you specifically what they think about the course so you can improve your course

Make sure feedback are anonymous

Use open questions to maximise information transfer

Formulate questions in a way so that delegates can give you constructive feedback rather than just some general positive feedback

24 Final Remarks

Knowing what to do is one thing, doing it is another. To develop new habits based on new knowledge, you need to treat training as a subject matter in its own right. Each time you deliver a course, reflect on your performance. What did you get right? What went wrong? What could have been better? What did the delegates think of your training? What new exercises or discussions should you cover when running the same course next time? You will need to make a note of all this while you are fresh as such details have the tendency to be forgotten very quickly.

Remember, the only way you can progress forward in your training skill is to measure yourself, compare your current performance with an ideal goal and then take actions to improve it.

We hope that this book, with its numerous exercises, has helped you to reflect on your training ability and know what to do next to become better at it. The learning does not stop with a single book though. It requires immersion and constant exposure. At SkillsConverged.com, we regularly publish articles and training materials that can enhance your training. Please consider subscribing to keep up-to-date in this highly valuable skill.

"Self-education is, I firmly believe, the only kind of education there is."

Isaac Asimov

Skills Converged

Appendix A: Training Plan Matrix

Appendix A: Training Plan Matrix

	Customer Service Skills	Leadership Skills	MS Power Point	Delegation Skills	Handling Difficult People	Handling Complaints	Decision Making
Trainer	Bill	Alan	Wen	Nancy	Sebastian	Krishna	Hugo
Admin Personnel							
Person 1	R, Training Course						O, Training Course
Person 2		R, Bite Sized	O: On-the-job-training	R: Online Training		R, Training Course	R, Training Course
Person 3							
Line Managers							
Person 4		R, Mentoring				R, Bite-Sized	
Person 5		R, Mentoring	R, Self-Study	R, Online training			
Person 6	R, Training Course	O, Self-Study	R, Self-Study		R, Training Course		R, Training Course
Marketing Team							
Person 7					R, Training Course	R, Training Course	

Notes:

R = Required: Required training

O = Optional: This usually depends on the availability of recourses or potential conflicts with possible important deadlines.

Training Types:

- *Training Course*
- *On-the-job training*
- *Online training*
- *Mentoring*
- *Self-Study.* Training activity can also be self-study where relevant materials are provided, such as books, on-line resources, software, tutorials, videos, etc.
- *Bite sized training.* Short courses or small training sessions

Schedule:

You can also add timing for each person's training requirements to schedule the training event. This can be added to each box.

Appendix A: Training Plan Matrix

	Customer Service Skills	Leadership Skills	MS Power Point	Delegation Skills	Handling Difficult People	Handling Complaints	Decision Making
Trainer							
Admin Personnel							
Person 1							
Person 2							
Person 3							
Line Managers							
Person 4							
Person 5							
Person 6							
Marketing Team							
Person 7							
Person 8							
Person 9							

Appendix B: Action Plan

Here is an example of a completed action plan:

Target Individuals	Training Activity	Delivery by Who	Delivery When	Delivery Where	Date Completed
Customer Service Skills Paul, Joseph	Training Course	Sahar	September 10th	In-House	September 10th
Leadership Skills William	Mentoring	Alex	Over the next 3 months	Office	
MS Power Point Anna, Erika, Mia	OnOLine Training	David	November 15th	Training Agency	
Delegation Skills Farida, Andrea	Training Course	Chloe	September 8th	Training Agency	September 8th
Handling Difficult People Louis, Andrea, Jan, Ahmad, William	Training Course	Ben, Chloe	October 10th and October 23rd	In-House	
3D Printing Machine Anna, Joseph	On-the-job training	Paul	During November	Workshop	

Target Individuals	Training Activity	Delivery by Who	Delivery When	Delivery Where	Date Completed
Training Topic 1					
Training Topic 2					
Training Topic 3					
Training Topic 4					
Training Topic 5					
Training Topic 6					
Training Topic 7					
Training Topic 8					
Training Topic 9					

Train the Trainer: The Art of Training Delivery

Appendix C: Solutions for Homework

Solutions for home work of Chapter 21 on handling group dynamics are provide here.

Scenario 1: They are in production phase

Scenario 2: They are in conflict phase

Scenario 3: They are in beginning phase

Scenario 4: They are in cohesion phase.

Scenario 5: How to handle:

> The group is in the beginning phase, approaching the conflict phase. In beginning phase people want to express their problems and influence the direction. Your role should to be to facilitate information exchange. Let everyone express their position to reduce the tension that will arise when people feel their views are not heard.
>
> Encourage those who are shy to talk more and reduce the domination of those who talk over others.
>
> As more information is exchanged, delegates may start to see similarities between their problems and issues which can lead them to abandon their original positions.

Next, focus on creating an environment of trust. You can achieve this by quickly going through a number of case studies, perhaps using examples from previous courses or problems that have been discussed in the past along with potential brief solutions. Your aim is to gradually gain delegate's confidence in your training and the fact that their problems are related both to the course and to other people's problems.

Appendix D: Recommended Reading

If you want to learn more on area covered here, consider the following recommended books:

On Accelerated Learning:
1. Best, B.J. (2003) *The Accelerated Learning Pocketbook*. Teachers' Pocketbooks.
2. Bransford, J.D., Brown, A.L. and Cocking, R. R. eds (2000) *How People Learn: brain, mind, experience and school*. National Academy Press.
3. Smith, A. (2002) *The Brain's Behind it: new knowledge about the brain and learning*. Network Educational Press.
4. Smith, A., Wise, D. and Lovatt, M. (2003) *Accelerated Learning: a user's guide*. Network Educational Press.

On Learning:

5. Duhigg, C. (2016) *"Smarter Faster Better: The Secrets of Being Productive"*, William Heinemann, ISBN-13: 978-0434023455
6. Ferriss, T., (2012) *"The 4-Hour Chef: The Simple Path to Cooking Like a Pro, Learning Anything, and Living the Good Life"*, Amazon Publishing, ISBN: 978-1477800072
7. Ericsson, K.A., Charness, N., Feltovich, P.J., Hoffman, R.R. (2006) *"The Cambridge Handbook of Expertise and Expert Performance"*, Cambridge University Press, ISBN: 978-0521600811
8. Buzan, T., (2009) *"The Mind Map Book: Unlock Your Creativity, Boost Your Memory, Change Your Life"*, BBC Active, ISBN: 978-1406647167
9. Duhigg, C. (2013) *"The Power of Habit: Why We Do What We Do, and How to Change"*, Random House Books, ISBN-13: 978-1847946249

On Motivation:

10. Skills Converged (2015) *"Focused Determination: How to Engineer Your Life to Maximise Your Happiness"*, ISBN: 978-1511730099
11. Pink, D.H., (2010) *"Drive: The Surprising Truth About What Motivates Us"*, Canongate Books, ISBN: 978-1847677686

References

Alter, A. L., & Oppenheimer, D. M. (2009) *"Uniting the tribes of fluency to form a metacognitive nation"*, Personality and Social Psychology Review, 13, 219-235.

Arias-Carrion O., Poppel, E. (2007) *"Dopamine, learning, and reward seeking behaviour"*, Acta Neurobiol Exp 2007, 67: 481-488.

Bengtsson, S.L., Dolan, R.J., Passingham, R.E, (2011) *"Priming for self-esteem influences the monitoring of one's own performance"*, Soc Cogn Affect Neurosci. Sep 2011; 6(4): 417-425.

Bernard, A.B, Moxnes, A., Yukiko, U.S., (2014) *"Geography and Firm Performance in the Japanese Production Network"*, Working paper No. 14034, National Bureau of Economic Research.

Buzan, T., Buzan, B. (2006) *"The Mind Map Book"*, BBC Active, ISBN: 978-1406612790.

Buzan, T. (2009) *"The Memory Book: How to Remember Anything You Want"*, BBC Active, ISBN: 978-1406644265

Cawood, J., Muller, F. B., Swartz, J. F. A. (1982) *"Grondbeginsels van die didaktiek"*.

Coyne, W.E., (2001) *"How 3m innovative for long-term growth"*, Research Technology Management 44, no. 2, 21-24

Diemand-Yauman, C., Oppenheimer, D.M., Vaughan, E.B., (2010) *"Fortune favors the Bold and the Italicized: Effects of disfluency on educational outcomes"*, Cognition (2010), doi:10.1016/j.cognition.2010.09.012

Duhigg, C., (2016) *"Smarter Faster Better: The Secrets of Being Productive in Life and Business"*, Random House.

Dukette, D., Cornish, D., (2009) *"The Essential 20: Twenty Components of an Excellent Health Care Team"*. RoseDog Books. pp. 72-73. ISBN 1-4349-9555-0.

Gardner, H. (1993) *"Frames of Mind: the theory of multiple intelligences"*, Bloomsbury

Goleman, D., (2013) *"Focus: The Hidden Driver of Excellence"*, Bloomsbury Publishing.

Greene, R. (2012) *"Mastery"*, Profile Books, ISBN-13: 978-1781250914

Johnson, D.W., and Johnson, R., (1988) *"Cooperation and competition theory and research"*, Edina, Minn.: Interaction Book Company

Lepper, M.R., Greene, D. & Nisbett, R.E. (1973) *"Undermining children's intrinsic interest with extrinsic reward: A test of the 'overjustification' hypothesis"*, Journal of personality and social psychology, 28(1), pp. 129-137.

Lozanov, G., (1970) *"Suggestopaedia - Desggestive Teaching Communicative Method on the Level of the Hidden Reserves of the Human Mind"*

Marshall, M. and Brown, J. (2006) *"Emotional reactions to achievement outcomes: Is it really best to expect the worst?"*, Cognition and Emotion, 2006, 20 (1), 43-63, Psychology Press Ltd.

Meier, D., (2000) *"The Accelerated Learning Handbook: A Creative Guide to Designing and Delivering Faster, More Effective Training Programs"*, McGraw-Hill Professional

Mueller, P.A., Oppenheimer, D. M., (2014) *"The Pen is Mightier than the Keyboard: Advantages of Longhand over Laptop Note Taking"*, Psychological Science, 25, no. 6.

Rose, C. (1985) *"Accelerated Learning."* Accelerated Learning Systems Ltd.

Schwartz, T., (2010) *"The Way We're Working Isn't Working: The Four Forgotten Needs That Energize Great Performance"* (Free Press, 2010) ISBN 9781439127667

Smith, A. (1996) *"Accelerated Learning in the Classroom Network Continuum Education"*, 4th edition, ISBN-13: 978-1855390348

Thompson, K. R., W. A. Hochwarter, N. J. Mathys. (1997) *"Stretch targets: What makes them effective?"* Academy of Management Executive. 11(3) 48-60.

Index

5

5-steps praise technique · 190

A

ABC questions · 182
Accelerated leaning · 158
Accelerated Learning · 27, 60
Action plan · 54
Active mode · 197
AL · 27
Alternating attention · 133
Anxiety · 217
Apprentice · 197
Asking questions · 179
Assessment and evaluation · 61
Attention span · 125

B

Backward perpendicular lines formation · 80
Barriers to learning · 62
Basal ganglia · 138
Beginning phase · 204
Boardroom configuration · 78
Body language · 154
Bottom-up · 138
Bounce · 213, 226
Bounce back · 183
Bounce to others · 183
Breaks · 281

C

CAB questions · 182
Chunking · 34, 129, 277
Circular formation · 80, 270
Circular table formation · 81, 270
Classroom configuration · 78
Clock Buddies · 99
Clock Buddies Tool · 268
Closed questions · 228
Cognitive disfluency · 143
Cognitive dissonance · 167
Cohesion phase · 205
Collaboration · 239
Competitive environment · 238
Computer · 69
Conclusion phase · 206
Confidence · 187
Conflict phase · 204
Conflicts · 100
Contextual learning · 31
Conversations · 266, 273
Credibility · 211
Criticism · 212, 246
Crossing arms · 105
Cycle of accelerated returns · 198

Train the Trainer: The Art of Training Delivery

D

Data-centric approach · 50
Deep observation · 196
Delegates · 14
Deliberate practice · 139
Didactic Principles · 60
Direct break · 130
Distractions · 99, 106
Divided attention · 134
Dominant delegates · 248
Domination · 206

E

Effective learning groups · 207
Embarrassment · 189
Emotional energy · 128
Empathy · 213
Energisers · 107
Engaging introductions · 171
Examples · 240
Exercises · 97
Expectation management · 113
Expectations · 111
Experimentation · 197
Eye contact · 105

F

Facilitating trainer · 21, 274
Facilitation · 20
Failed experiments · 141
Feedback form · 44, 284
First impressions · 234
Flipchart · 68
Focus · 108

G

Gain Time · 212
Gap of disappointment · 120
Group exercises formation · 82
Group questions · 182

H

Half circle formation · 81
Humour · 171

I

Indirect break · 130
Individual learning · 238
Individualisation · 60
Informal chat formation · 83
Instinct · 139
Interactive boards · 69
Internet access · 69
Interview position · 82
Intimidation · 100
Intrinsic motivation · 126

J

Jargon · 151, 261
Joy · 126

L

Laptop · 68
Learner · 14
Learner-centred · 264
Learning · 162, 196
Lecture · 88, 159, 160, 161
Lecturing trainer · 21
Lighting · 71
Lived experience · 61

M

Mental energy · 128
Methodicalness · 60
Mistakes · 141, 153
Mnemonic · 241
Modalities · 28
Morphy's law · 254
Motivation · 157

O

Open questions · 181
Organised rule · 69
Overjustification effect · 142
Overwhelmed · 98

P

Pace · 108
Participant · 14
Passive Mode · 196
Physical energy · 128
Physical environment · 30
Poor expressions · 152
Practice mode · 197
Praise · 186, 189, 242, 244
Praise sandwich · 246
Pre-emptive approach · 214
Production phase · 205
Projector · 267
Projectors · 68
Psychological environment · 30
Purposefulness · 60

Q

Questioning · 159

R

Receiving mode · 72
Redicule · 226
Reflect · 171, 213
Relay questions · 182
Results-oriented · 31
Return on Investment · 120
Rewards · 142
Ridicule · 214
ROI · 120

S

Selective attention · 132
Self-activity · 61
Self-concept · 115
Self-discovery · 236

Silence · 87, 180
Skill acquisition · 196
Skills · 121
Skills gap analysis · 49
Slides · 255, 260
SMART goals · 117
Socialisation · 60
Spiritual energy · 128
Stories · 165
Storytelling · 166
Struggle · 98
Student · 14
Suggestopedia · 28
Summary sandwich · 152
Sustained attention · 132

T

Tacit knowledge · 196
Taking Over · 207
Taster session · 159
Team building exercises · 90
Theory of Multiple Intelligences · 28
Tickable task · 121
Time management · 224
Timetable · 267
Tipping point · 198
TNA · 39, 49, 52, Training Needs Analysis
Top-down · 138
Touch · 229
Trainee · 14
Trainer centred approach · 20
Trainer script · 69
Training environment · 154, 171, 190, 215, 217, 229, 267
Training Needs Analysis · 39, 49, 63
Training plan · 53
Two perpendicular lines formation · 80

U

U Formation · 79

V

Ventilation · 72
Vision · 229

W

Whiteboard · 67
Withdrawal · 206

About Skills Converged

Skills Converged is based in the United Kingdom and specialises in the design and development of soft skills training courses as well as providing various courses and books on training trainers. Our training materials are used world-wide by the training community to train some of the world's most prestigious and successful organisations. As course designers of personal and interpersonal skills, we are passionate to learn what it takes to provide effective training with long lasting results. Our books written for the general public are designed as self-study courses based on the same principles of learning that we use to produce our successful training courses. Our self-help books are suitable for anyone interested in improving their personal and people skills.

For more information please check www.SkillsConverged.com

About Ethan Honary

Skills Converged was founded by Dr. Ethan (Ehsan) Honary in 2008. He is a training specialist with years of experience in the training industry. He has an interest in a diverse set of subjects such as psychology, artificial intelligence, social sciences, business management, fine arts, computer graphics and software engineering. Through Skills Converged, Ethan has enabled thousands of trainers worldwide to deliver outstanding training courses on soft skills and has empowered people to realise their full potential. He is an advocate of using the latest training methodologies that help speed up training while simultaneously make learning last longer.

Printed in Great Britain
by Amazon